A WICCAN
HERBAL

A WICCAN HERBAL

Healing secrets of natural magic

MARIE RODWAY

quantum

LONDON · NEW YORK · TORONTO · SYDNEY

quantum

The Publishing House, Bennetts Close,
Cippenham, Berkshire, SL1 5AP, England.

ISBN 0-572-02340-5

Typeset by ABM Typographics Ltd, Hull
Printed in Great Britain by St. Edmundsbury Press, Bury, St. Edmunds, Suffolk

CONTENTS

FOREWORD

While leafing through my collection of herbals I realised there did not appear to have been one written from the Wiccan viewpoint. This book is an attempt to remedy the situation.

The book contains a collection of recipes and snippets of knowledge about herbs given to me by a number of Wiccans – the old (and current) name for witches. Wiccans are among the most knowledgeable people on earth about herbalism, an art they call 'wortcunning'. They have, however, tended to keep this knowledge to themselves, so this anthology affords a rare insight into a world that has been kept secret for many centuries.

The Wiccans who have contributed to this book are a mixture of people: some I knew and had had contact with, others I approached because they had interesting angles on Wicca; some work as sole Wiccans, others are involved in groups.

The book contains a mixture of remedies, some of which may be safely tried by the reader and others which are included for interest only, or perhaps for mentioning to your qualified herbalist. Some use the most workaday ingredients, such as apples or honey; others use plants which seldom feature in herbals, for example hemlock (a cup of which killed Socrates) and black nightshade. Many of the more unusual herbs mentioned are either poisonous or have powerful side-effects. Clear warnings are given about experimenting with these; their use must be left to qualified professionals.

There are, however, plenty of remedies that can be tried out with impunity, for example those using apples and honey mentioned above, elderflowers and elderberries, nettles (whose most notable side-effect is acting as a laxative if picked after midsummer!), blackberries, cider vinegar, peppermint (for digestive problems) and sage leaves, rubbed on to clean teeth and strengthen gums. Another natural tooth cleaner is the strawberry.

The emphasis throughout the book is on the solitary Wiccan rather than on group work. It points the way towards practising the old arts of Wicca, without dwelling on group worship and ritual, which can have negative connotations. The vast majority of these remedies will be of interest to someone working alone; you do not need to be part of a group.

Incidentally, one of the tips given to me was to keep a pot of basil on the kitchen windowsill to keep the room clear of flies. It works wonderfully well: the few flies that found their way into my kitchen this summer were unhappy insects who couldn't wait to be 'liberated' through an open window!

I found the task of putting this book together quite fascinating. I hope you enjoy reading it as much.

Marie Rodway

ACKNOWLEDGEMENTS

I should like to thank all the Wiccans who have so generously contributed to this volume. It could not have come into existence without them. They took a great deal of trouble to provide me with information, and I am most grateful.

Particular thanks are extended to Keith Morgan for kind permission to reproduce his piece 'Good Sense and Incense' as Chapter 6.

I also received much assistance from my husband, Howard, for which many thanks. These are due not least because, in the first instance, he allowed me to borrow from his precious collection of occult books!

HOW TO USE
THIS BOOK

The remedies in this book are intended to be of general interest, but should only be used by skilled herbalists with the knowledge to diagnose ailments, select appropriate remedies and decide on dosages. Many herbs have powerful properties, and to experiment with them without relevant knowledge and expertise is dangerous.

Warnings about the danger of using certain very powerful herbs are included with the individual herbs.

It is most important to consult a doctor about all but the most trivial medical problems, and always do so if symptoms are severe or persist. Never guess what is wrong and treat an ailment without expert assistance. These remedies are intended as adjuncts to conventional medicine, not replacements.

PLEASE NOTE:

General principles for making remedies
Refer to Chapter 2 for guidance on acquiring and storing herbs, and for detailed instructions on making teas, infusions, decoctions, syrups, ointments, poultices and compresses. An infusion is less concentrated than a decoction, so you may wish to try an infusion first.

Proportions are of great importance in these remedies, so observe the following:

Cup: where this measure is mentioned in recipes, it refers to a standard teacup, which holds about 250 ml/8 fl oz/1 cup.

Grain: 1 grain = 0.065 g

Ratio of fresh to dried herbs: where both can be used, the rule of thumb is to use a ratio of 3:1 fresh to dried herbs. Where using American cup measures, herbs should be fairly tightly packed.

Dosages: The usual herbal tea dose is 25 g/1 oz of fresh herbs or 20 ml/1 heaped tbsp of dried herbs to 600 ml/1 pt/ 2½ cups of water.

Dosages for children
4–7 years: quarter the adult dose
8–12 years: half the adult dose

How to store remedies
Always decant herbal remedies such as syrups and ointments into completely sterile screw-top jars. To sterilise glass containers, submerge them in clean water and boil *gently* for 10 minutes (since heat can make glass shatter). A safer method is to use a proprietary brand of baby bottle steriliser. Follow the instructions on the label.

Containers for herbal teas and decoctions should be as clean as possible, but as tea is made with boiling water and drunk the same day, and decoctions are boiled for quite a while, sterilisation is not essential in these cases. If a decoction is to be stored, however, a sterile container should be used.

Storage jars should be made of coloured glass so that less light reaches the remedy. It is also best if bottles are kept in a dark cupboard.

＊ 1 ＊

AN INTRODUCTION
TO WITCHCRAFT

Herbalism is deeply rooted in witchcraft and herbal
knowledge has always been one of the skills of the
Craft.

It has been said that witchcraft – or Wicca, as it was
called long ago and now is again – is one of the most ancient
religions in the world and also one of the youngest. Its roots
are buried deep in the Old Religion, the worship of nature
and its hidden forces that began in prehistoric times.

The earliest deity was almost certainly female, a
Goddess of Magic and Fertility who was capable of creating
new life both from her own body and from the apparent des-
olation of the land in winter. Another of her many names
was Mother Nature, and witches today still believe that our
planet is itself the body of the Goddess, so that anyone dam-
aging it is harming the Great Mother herself.

Consort of the Great Goddess was the Horned God of
Death and Hunting. Cave paintings show him leading the
great hunts of the times, clothed in animal skins and with
antlers on his head. In prehistoric days brave young men
would have dressed in this way to mingle with the herds of
beasts, so that the chosen prey could be singled out and
despatched, perhaps by being driven over a precipice. The
Horned God has sometimes been depicted with two cres-
cent-shaped horns on his head rather than antlers, and these
are thought to denote his special relationship with the moon.
He has no connection with the devil of the much-later
Christian Church.

The Great Goddess ruled over the green part of the year

from spring to when the leaves wither; hence another of her names: the Green Goddess. The Horned God reigned through the winter months, beginning at Hallowe'en. Together they represented the opposites of male and female, light and darkness, positive and negative and the sun and the moon.

The Green Man is an aspect of the Horned God. He was the God of the Woodlands and the spirit of trees and growing plants. Carvings of him in stone or wood can sometimes be seen in remote northern corners of cathedrals and old churches; they usually show a man's face looking out from a frame of (sacred) oak leaves.

The Wiccan philosophy consists of four main strands: the worship of the old gods and goddesses and nature; magic (spells); divination (psychic powers), and healing (principally herbalism).

THE MOON IN MAGIC

Although Wiccans do not worship the moon as such, it is to them the magical symbol of the ancient Goddess of Enchantment, Mystery, Love and Fruitfulness, and much witchcraft is lunar magic. The moon is so closely connected with the fertility of women – and to a lesser extent of men – that it was totally natural for witches to turn to the White Goddess, an aspect of the Great Goddess who is represented by the moon, for help with their magic. In prehistoric times, when the moon was regarded as one of the most powerful sources of fruitfulness (of herds, harvests and human reproduction), it was believed that moonbeams made women pregnant and those who wished for children used to sleep outside, in the light of the moon.

The pattern of 13 lunar cycles to the year is the basis of the special occult affinity with that number. Esbats, the monthly meetings of covens, take place when the moon is full. Magical power is considered to be at its greatest at full moon, hence the old rhyme, passed down through the generations by word of mouth:

> 'Pray to the moon when she is round,
> Luck with you will then abound.

What you seek for shall be found,
On the sea or solid ground.'

The moon is regarded as being essentially feminine, the sun as masculine. Witches, the majority of whom were – and still are – female, believe that it gave its white light to be their own colour.

The metal silver, associated with the moon as it shares its colour, reputedly protects against evil spirits and enhances psychic powers. It has always been much favoured for making amulets, and many Wiccans today wear silver jewellery, often in the form of a pentacle pendant or ring. The pentacle, a five-pointed star with a single point at the top, ✩, is the symbol of witchcraft, as the cross is of Christianity. It represents both the Old Religion and the craft of magic.

A NEUTRAL CRAFT

Witches say their magic is in itself neither black nor white but neutral in colour and capable of being used for either good or bad purposes. No sensible Wiccan would, however, wish harm on anyone else, since all believe in the Threefold Law of Return: 'What good you do returns to you threefold; what harm you do also returns to you threefold'.

RAISING THE POWER

Wiccans' power to perform magic utilises the forces of nature, and is raised mainly by dancing in a circle, perhaps around a tree or bonfire. These dances usually begin as jolly, country-style measures and develop into something much wilder and more uninhibited. Witches believe that their magical power comes from their own bodies and is more accessible if they are naked or 'skyclad'. Another method of raising power is by rhythmic chanting; the mantra 'Hare Krishna' is an example of this from another tradition.

Magic was originally used for simple objectives such as rainmaking, ensuring the fertility of cattle and a good harvest. It was performed by the priestesses of the Goddess, who were also the leaders of the tribe's magic rites and its prophetesses. Later on they were called Wise Ones and then witches.

CHRISTIANITY TAKES OVER

A wave of masculine feeling built up against the supremacy of the Great Goddess and her priestesses, however, around 1800–1500 BC, when Abraham, the first Hebrew prophet, is believed to have lived in Canaan. Men began to become priests and then fill the chief positions. They glorified physical strength and combat. More and more emphasis was placed on male deities, until the Hebrew prophet Abraham introduced the concept of a single, patriarchal God. Gradually the Old Religion was displaced.

By the time of the Roman Empire, black witchcraft (that thought to be harmful) was considered a crime punishable by torture and death. On the other hand white witches (whose activities consisted mainly of healing and divination) and sorcerers (who principally cast spells and provided charms to bring health, wealth, love, and so on) were considered acceptable.

During the so-called Dark Ages, from the fifth to the early eleventh century AD, it is thought that in Britain Christianity and the Old Religion existed side by side, though while the young Church of Christ gradually gained in strength, the earlier beliefs waned. Wiccans were then the respected wise women of rural communities, with an important role in their villages. Their knowledge of natural phenomena made them valuable weather forecasters to those who grew crops – nearly everyone at that time. They were also the village spellcasters, interpreters of dreams, psychologists, midwives and herbalists-cum-healers. Each village had its own wise woman.

During this time Christian churches were often built on pagan sites, such as Sacred Groves, and included altars to the Old Gods, usually in their northern corners. When the Catholic Church began oppressing followers of the Old Religion, from about 1050, it sealed up the north doors of churches and converted most of the pagan shrines into Lady Chapels – replacing the Great Goddess with the Holy Mother. Followers of the old ways went underground.

PERSECUTION – A LONG TRADITION

There followed a long period of the most cruel persecution of witches – and of many people who were not witches at all – that lasted from the thirteenth to the seventeenth centuries and is called by Wiccans 'The Burning Times'. Nobody knows how many victims were tortured and killed, but it is thought to have been between 150,000 and 200,000, with 100,000 of them burned at the stake in Germany where witch-hunting was particularly savage. Some estimates are, however, much higher.

Both the Catholic and Protestant Churches proclaimed that witches were heretics who had renounced Christ and made a pact with the devil. They saw witches' sabbats as evil occasions. Sabbats are the eight festivals of the year that witches observe, and were once pagan celebrations. They mark the changing of the seasons and the agricultural year. They are happy occasions at which witches dance, feast and generally make merry, honouring the Goddess and her Horned God, and giving thanks for all that the earth provides, since Wicca is above all a religion of fertility.

The churches said witches rode to their sabbats on broomsticks, sacrificed children at these festivals, held orgies with demons and used their magic power to raise storms, revenge themselves on enemies and perpetrate other evils.

There is little evidence to support these charges, some of which were the same accusations that had been levelled many times in the past at religious minorities, for example by the Syrians against the Jews and by the Romans against the Christians.

All that we have from that time is a pitiful collection of 'confessions' extracted under the most barbaric torture from those who fell into the hands of the Papal Inquisition or opportunists such as the Englishman Matthew Hopkins, known as the 'Witch-Finder General', who collected a large fee for every witch put to death.

This brutal repression took place not in the so-called Dark Ages, as is popularly believed, but during the Renaissance and Reformation while, as Jeffrey Russell says in his *History of Witchcraft*, 'Leonardo painted, Palestrina composed and Shakespeare wrote'.

One result of the persecution is that witchcraft has become confused in the minds of many with Satanism and what the witch-hunters called devil worship. This is one reason why members of the Craft today prefer to be called Wiccans. It is evident now that some aspects of devil worship so many people were accused of never existed. For instance, is it really believable that witches flew through the air to their sabbats on broomsticks with, some said, candles perched at one end to light their way?

What they may have done is to rub on to their skin, especially at pulse points, salves containing hallucinogenic herbs – the famous 'witches' flying ointments' – that resulted in fantastic out-of-body experiences: what spiritualists refer to as 'astral travelling'.

Recipes for these flying ointments were – and are – secret, but a little information is available. Research was carried out some time ago by Dr Erich-Will Peuckert of the University of Göttingen in Germany. He made up an unguent based on ingredients listed in a book entitled *De Miraculus Rerum Naturalium* by Giovanni Porta, which first appeared in 1560. Experiments on himself and a friend proved, he said, that the ointment was spectacularly effective. This salve used hog's lard as a base and contained thornapple, henbane, deadly nightshade, wild celery and parsley. **WARNING!** Most of these herbs are highly poisonous and it would be very dangerous to experiment with them.

Another recipe was given to the Wiccan writer Doreen Valiente. It is said to have been used by a modern witch, but no information is available on its effects. Using a base of beeswax, lanoline and almond oil, the ingredients are listed as aconite, poppy juice, foxglove, poplar leaves and cinquefoil. Again, these are not herbs for the amateur; only skilled herbalists should have any dealings with them.

More details of Giovanni Porta's recipes for flying ointments and of Dr Peuckert's research are to be found in Doreen Valiente's book *An ABC of Witchcraft Past and Present* (Robert Hale, 1973, 1984).

Also of interest may be one of the formulae for flying ointments given in *The Witch Cult in Western Europe* by Margaret Murray (published 1921), a book famous in occult circles. Ingredients are: fat, juice of water parsnip, aconite, cinquefoil, deadly nightshade and soot. **Remember**, several of them are very poisonous, so please leave any experiments to the experts.

Some other equally wild accusations levelled at witches in the past were that they sacrificed unbaptised children in their rites (a horror story spread by the Church to frighten parents into having their babies christened without delay), and that they summoned the devil himself to their sabbats, when he often appeared as a goat. The latter piece of foolishness may have been based on the fact that the male leader of a coven sometimes donned animal skins and antlers to represent the Horned God.

CHARGES OF SATANISM

These and similar stories, particularly as they frequently featured in the 'confessions' of victims of the witch-hunters, resulted in a widespread belief in the Middle Ages that witches were in league with Satan. This gradually faded as changes in philisophical and religious thought took place, and witchcraft eventually became regarded as outdated superstition believed only by the poorly educated. Nevertheless, rumours and sometimes more substantial information about devil worship appeared from time to time. In the seventeenth century, black masses were said to have been conducted by corrupt priests: one notorious case involved a mistress of King Louis XIV of France. A black mass is a parody of the Catholic holy mass, in which the devil is worshipped. Various elements of the mass are reversed, for example the cross is inverted, parts of the mass are performed backwards, and black is substituted for white, black candles being burned, for example. Black masses are performed by Satanists, and Satanism, sometimes called the left-hand or sinister path, has no connection with Wicca.

Madame de Montespan, mistress of Louis XIV, is said to

have organised the performance of black masses by an occultist called La Voisin and a womanising priest, the Abbé Guiborg, which involved magical and sexual rites.

A hundred years later there was Sir Francis Dashwood's Hellfire Club whose members were thought to be Satanists. However, their meetings consisted of nothing more sinister than bouts of heavy drinking and general wild behaviour often involving women they called 'nuns'.

Later the Church of Carmel was founded in France by the Satanist Abbé Bouillan, and the Society for the Reparation of Souls formed by his friend Eugene Vintras. Both organisations are thought to have celebrated the black mass.

Today Satanism is said to be practised by a small number of people. In Europe the movement is known as 'traditional Satanism' and is represented by such groups as the Satanic Order of the Nine Angles. This organisation sets out its main aims as 'magical adepthood' and 'the development of individual consciousness'. It stresses that its rites involve no criminal activities. In American the Dark Tradition derives from the (relatively modern) Church of Satan founded in California by Anton LaVey. This cult is said to concentrate on the glorification of the ego and celebrations of the pleasures of life. LaVey, however, makes a point of emphasising that there is no reverence of evil or criminal behaviour.

There remain accounts of Satanic ritual abuse that have persistently circulated on both sides of the Atlantic. Hard evidence to support them has proved very difficult to find. Followers of the main branches of Satanism deny any involvement. Wiccans have steadfastly maintained that they have no connection whatsoever with devil worship in any form. So, if the stories are true, who is responsible? One of the principal theories, supported by American author Rosemary Guiley, is that there may be a few groups of evil people who falsely call themselves Satanists and prey on runaway children and vagrants. In Britain, the opinion of the Sub-Culture Alternatives Freedom Foundation, an organisation aiming to safeguard the right of everyone to freedom of religion, is that the Satanic abuse stories are updated versions of the old devil worship tales with which the witch-hunters were so obsessed, but this time spread by Christian fundamentalists. It states that no occultist has ever been prosecuted for any child abuse crime, and that there is no proof that such things occur.

LITTLE WRITTEN HISTORY

Very little witch lore has been documented down the centuries, partly because in the past few Wiccans could read or write, and partly because to possess such evidence of involvement in the Craft was so dangerous. Knowledge was usually passed on by word of mouth; in the case of a witch family, from parent to child, or from a Wiccan of one sex to an initiate of the other where a newcomer to a coven was concerned.

Today many witches keep a personal handwritten book called a *Book of Shadows* in which they record a selection of beliefs, rituals, herbal lore, chants, charms and other information that has special meaning for them. A few witches kept such books in the old days, then called a black book, but the tradition is that when a witch passes on the book is burned, so not many have survived.

THE CRAFT GOES UNDERGROUND

By the end of the witch-hunts the Craft of the Wise in Britain and the rest of Western Europe had become invisible and had formed itself into small secret pockets, some of which still exist today. In England, for example, parts of Shropshire are well known for their 'witchy' communities, as are certain Cotswold localities.

However, in spite of witches increasingly being left in peace, the village wise woman never fully regained her former position in the community. This was largely due to the Industrial Revolution, when many people moved to towns and cities where there was work for them in the new factories, and the first advances occurred in the development of modern medicine. Progress in scientific knowledge also put Wicca in an unfashionable light. The old ways came to be regarded as a collection of misty, primitive, superstitious beliefs that no modern-thinking person could possibly take seriously.

The Victorian era saw a revival of interest in the occult in the form of spiritualism. Thousands of mediums claimed to be able to contact spirits 'on the other side' and see into the future. Some were genuine; many were frauds.

THE CRAFT TODAY

Modern witchcraft came into being during the years following the Second World War. One of the first indications was the appearance in 1948 of a book called *The White Goddess* by Robert Graves. This described an ancient cult devoted to a goddess of the moon and poetry which Graves declared had existed throughout Europe long ago, especially among Celtic peoples. The book was enormously influential in occult circles.

Soon afterwards a Wiccan called Gerald Gardner (1884–1964), who had first been initiated into a coven of hereditary witches in the New Forest in the 1930s, began writing about the Craft. Among his works were a novel *High Magic's Aid* (1949) and the non-fiction *Witchcraft Today* (1954). The rituals and other materials that appear in his writings – derived partly from his first coven and augmented by material invented by himself and another well-known witch, Doreen Valiente – form the basis of what has come to be known as the Gardnerian tradition of witchcraft, one of the two main branches of the modern cult.

The other is called Alexandrian, after its founder Alexander Sanders (1926–88). He was a much more flamboyant character than his fellow Englishman Gardner. He called himself the 'King of the Witches', to the annoyance of many in the Craft, as there is no such position. He was, however, said to have been a genuinely gifted psychic and healer. His teachings are similar to those of Gardner, and it is said that after being refused entry to several Gardnerian covens he managed to obtain a copy of their *Book of Shadows* and based his own tradition on that. The writer Stewart Farrar, who was initiated into the Craft by him, says that

Alex Sanders has nevertheless made a valuable contribution to modern witchcraft.

In addition to the two main modern branches of Wicca, the isolation of many witch groups has resulted in the Craft developing in a wide variety of ways. There are, for example, hereditary witches who claim that their families have secretly practised the Craft for many centuries. Dianic witchcraft, named after Diana, the Roman Goddess of the Moon and the Hunt, is mainly popular in the United States of America and has a strong feminist slant. Celtic witchcraft is quite different, being based on the old myths, rites and beliefs of those peoples. Their deities are still called by their Celtic names. An example of this branch of the Craft is Cylch Cyhiraeth, the coven in North Wales which has contributed a number of remedies to this book.

TWENTIETH-CENTURY WITCHES

So what are twentieth-century witches like? There are no standard patterns, of course, especially as Wiccans tend to be free and independent-minded spirits who follow their own star regardless of the opinions of others. Indeed, one of the few laws of the Craft is the Wiccan Rede:

> 'Eight words the Wiccan Rede fulfil,
> An' it harm none, do what ye will!'

However, there are often clues that will point an outsider in the direction of the Craft. Although there are some 'city witches', many have a marked affinity for wild places, the countryside, flowers (more often than not with their roots still attached, rather than cut) and animals. Their household pets, which may be 'familiars' who assist in divination, tend to be complete (un-neutered and therefore capable of reproduction) as the Old Religion was after all a fertility cult. Often there are a number of unusual objects in their homes, such as besoms, an ancient symbol of witchcraft connected with the old crop-raising dances, strangely wrought candlesticks and a pack of Tarot cards or perhaps some rune stones.

Most modern Wiccans, sometimes called neo-pagan

witches, still worship the Great Goddess and the Horned God of the Old Religion. Magic remains an important part of their cult, as does the development of psychic abilities. They believe there is nothing supernatural or diabolical about the latter: everyone possesses these capabilities but not many are aware of them.

Today magic is directed at the spiritual development of witches themselves. It can of course be used for such activities as foretelling the future, influencing others and contacting spirits, but the main intention is to become more evolved as human beings by furthering their magic powers. If they can do this, witches believe they are contributing to the progress of the human race.

While some of their old roles – village midwife for one – no longer exist, others are still much in demand. People remain eager to see into the future, for instance, and Wiccans who are willing to tell fortunes are assured of a stream of clients. Witches are also often notable psychic healers and diviners of water and other substances.

HARNESSING THE POWER OF HERBS

Herbal knowledge, which they call Wortcunning, has always been one of the skills of the Craft. Although it might be thought that their expertise as medicinal herbalists is as out of date as the application of leeches to bring down a fever, many do not agree. Herbs really do have medicinal properties: it is well known, for example, that digitalis, prescribed by doctors today for some kinds of heart disease, comes from the foxglove; that eucalyptus oil will ease coughs and colds; and – one that has only recently come to the fore – that feverfew is very effective in helping migraine sufferers. Herbalism is very much alive today and its practice is widespread.

Apart from their medicinal uses, herbs are also said to have magical properties. St John's Wort is believed to repel evil spirits, and the rowan tree to guard against malevolent spells, which is why Romany gypsies carry walking sticks made from this wood. The flowers of the periwinkle, sometimes called sorcerer's violet, protect against evil and are used in love spells. Honeysuckle flowers when picked and placed in a vase will bring luck; lightly bruised and rubbed on the forehead, the fresh flowers will also enhance psychic capabilities. A species of willow herb, whose country name is 'enchanter's nightshade', is another magical plant.

Wiccans believe that herbs used for magical purposes should be gathered according to the phases of the moon. Where they are to be used for spells of a constructive, building nature, they should be collected while the moon waxes; where removal of an obstacle or a bad feeling directed towards you is required, pick your plants during a waning moon. The Dark of the Moon is the time to find herbs for dark magic. Witches rarely use this, believing that wishing ill-fortune on others will bring it rebounding on themselves, but very occasionally they will utilise their powers to try and stop negative activity of one kind or another, such as a series of crimes.

Where herbs are to be used for magic, some witches say they should be gathered at the hour of the day which corresponds to the planet that rules them astrologically. If you would like to know more about this tradition you will find the astrological rulerships (Mars, Saturn, Mercury, Venus and Jupiter, plus the sun and moon) of many herbs in the famous old Culpeper Herbal, *Culpeper's Complete Herbal and English Physician*, first published in 1652. More are listed in the American book *Cunningham's Encyclopedia of Magical Herbs* (Llewellyn Publications, 1985). One source of a table of planetary hours is *Spells and How They Work* by Janet and Stewart Farrar (Robert Hale, 1990).

A word of warning!

The recipes in this herbal all originate from Wiccan sources and include as much information as possible. It is hoped that all readers will find them interesting, but they are intended to be of practical use only to skilled herbalists who have the knowledge to diagnose ailments, select appropriate medicines and decide on dosages, etc. Many herbs possess powerful properties and experimenting with them without the relevant expertise is dangerous. Please do not try.

It is also very important to consult a general practitioner or other doctor about all but trivial medical problems. No one should gamble with his or her health by taking a guess at what is wrong and treating an ailment without expert assistance.

❧ 2 ❧

AN INTRODUCTION
TO HERBALISM

Newcomers to the world of medicinal herbalism may like to know a little about obtaining herbs and how a few sprigs of this or that can be turned into a medicine.

WHERE TO FIND YOUR PLANTS

There are three main ways of acquiring these plants: by growing them in a garden, gathering them in the countryside, or buying them ready dried from a shop.

You do not need a great deal of space to grow at least a selection of herbs at home. A small flower bed, reasonably sunny and sheltered, is perfectly adequate; alternatively, herbs can be mixed in with vegetables or ornamental flowers anywhere in the garden. Sometimes this even has a beneficial effect: if rue is planted in a vegetable plot, for example, it will keep cats away from the newly-prepared earth they so love.

Herb seeds can be bought from many shops and garden centres; the latter often stock young plants too. One of the most famous shops in the field of herbalism is Culpeper's, which has 20 branches in England: these can be found in the Source List on page 112, together with the address of their Mail Order Department. If difficulty is experienced in obtaining seeds, a wide range is sold by a number of specialist firms; the Source List gives the names and addresses of some of these companies.

WHEN TO SOW

Myrddin Einion, High Priest of a coven in North Wales called Cylch Cyhiraeth, gives the following information on the phases of the moon Wiccans believe are the most beneficial for planting herb seeds. The best time to put in any seeds is when the seventh moon after Hallowe'en is shining. Always sow during the waxing moon, except for herbs whose roots are to be used: the time to sow these is when the moon is waning. Herbs grown for their flowers and fragrance should be planted when the moon is in an air sign of the zodiac. Herbs for spiritual purposes/consciousness need to be started when the moon is in a water sign. Herbs to be used for their healing properties should be planted when the moon is in a fire sign. The ideal time to sew herbs grown for nutritional reasons is when the moon is in an earth sign.

For those who wish to go out into the countryside and pick their own herbs, a good reference book to help with identification is essential. There are many available; one of the best is *The Concise British Flora in Colour* by W. Keble Martin.

WHERE TO LOOK

When gathering plants, give the verges of busy roads a wide berth; pollutants from passing vehicles may well have affected anything growing there. Try and find the herbs you need in more remote areas that are not adjacent to farmland on which pesticides may have been sprayed. Only the tips of a plant should be taken: these are in any case the most suitable for herbal preparations, and leaving the main stems intact will enable the plant to continue to grow. If you are in any doubt about the identity of something you have picked, don't use it unless you can get an expert second opinion. Never pick rare plants, but whatever you do pick, leave enough of the plant intact for re-growth to take place.

If this seems a bit disheartening, the beginner can always gather plants about which there can be no possible mistake, such as stinging nettles, dandelions and elderberries.

WHEN TO GATHER

As a general rule, blossoms and leaves should be collected in spring and early summer, fruit and berries in late summer, and roots in the autumn.

HOW TO DRY PLANTS

To dry plants, hang them up in small bunches or lay them loosely on racks of muslin or cheesecloth in a warm, dry place with a good current of air. Store the dried plants in airtight containers in a dark place such as a cupboard.

THEN GET TO WORK

Tea or infusion?

Once you have your herbs, there are many ways of turning them into medicines. The simplest method is to make an infusion, which is like brewing a pot of tea. Flowers and leaves should be used, either fresh or dried. Keep a special pot for the purpose, as lingering traces of herbs will affect the flavour of ordinary tea (and vice versa). In some recipes the word 'tea' is used, rather than 'infusion' – an infusion of hyssop is usually called hyssop tea, for example – but the meaning is the same. If using fresh plants, slightly crush the leaves/flowers to release more of their juices. Three handfuls of a fresh plant or one handful of a dried plant to 600 ml/1 pt/2½ cups water is the usual dose; allow the infusion to steep for at least half an hour. It may be drunk in small amounts through the day, either warm or cold.

Decoction

A decoction, which is more concentrated than an infusion, is where the plant (leaves, flowers or root) is covered with water and then boiled until the volume of the liquid is halved. Where roots are used, 25 g/1 oz of dried root or 75 g /3 oz of fresh root is covered with 600 ml/1 pt/2½ cups of water. If the roots are thick, they should be sliced lengthways. A decoction is normally taken as a small cupful three times a day.

Herbal syrup

A herbal syrup is where 225 g/8 oz/³⁄₄ cup of honey is added to 600 ml/1 pt/2¹⁄₂ cups of an infusion. The mixture is boiled until it thickens.

Ointment

Ointment is made by crushing 50 g/2 oz of a dried herb (using a pestle and mortar) and mixing it with 225 g/8 oz/ 1 cup of melted petroleum jelly. Simmer for 20 minutes, strain and store in a screw-top jar. An ointment is for external use only.

Poultice

A poultice is made from crushed herbs and a piece of cloth. Wrap the herbs in the material, immerse in boiling water for a few minutes, squeeze out the excess liquid and apply to the affected area.

Compress

A compress is where a cloth is soaked in a cold herbal infusion, then gently wrung out and laid on the part to be treated.

If children are to be given herbal medicine, the doses for them are normally the following: half the adult dose for an average-sized child aged 8–12 and a quarter of the adult dose for a child aged 4–7.

3

SINGLE-HERB
REMEDIES: 'SIMPLES'

Herbs can be used as remedies for all manner of complaints and disorders, from skin problems to indigestion, from burns and scalds to winter colds, to ease sleeplessness or help a hangover. You can also use them in beauty preparations, as a hair tint or a face cream, for example.

The vast majority of remedies in this chapter are 'simples', which means they are made from single herbs.

The herbs are presented in alphabetical order for easy reference and include general information on the herbs and how to use them.

Some of the remedies are for teas, infusions or syrups, others for ointments, poultices or compresses. Remember to refer back to Chapter 2, pages 27–28, for general instructions for making these preparations.

Warning!
Some of the herbs are very powerful and should only be used with extreme caution. Where this applies, warnings appear with the individual entries.

ACONITE *Aconitum napellus*

Warning!
Aconite contains one of the most powerful known poisons, therefore expert assistance should be sought before any contact with it. Even the smallest amount of the plant's juice entering a break in the skin can be fatal. The utmost caution must be exercised.

---

aconite

This herb was one of the traditional ingredients used by witches for making 'flying ointments'. It is also associated with the Moon Goddess Hecate. Aconite, often called monkshood, is a deadly poison which acts with great speed. It has been applied to the tips of spears, darts and arrows for centuries. Every part of the plant is toxic, the root in particular. It is safest not to grow aconite in the kitchen garden at all as it has on occasion been mistaken for horseradish, with tragic results.

The herb has anodyne properties when applied externally, and preparations such as aconite liniment and ointment have in the past been rubbed into the skin to relieve the pain of neuralgia, sciatica and rheumatism.

AGRIMONY *Agrimonia eupatoria*

(TANNIN) *COCKLEBUR*

For jaundice, liver and blood complaints.
Agrimony will purify the blood when taken as a drink. When applied as a lotion, it cleanses the skin. Mixed with equal parts of red wine it is an effective antidote to snake bites.

Preparation and dosage: pour 600 ml/1 pt/ 2½ cups of boiling water on to 3 handfuls of the fresh herb or one of the dried. Let this infuse for 10 minutes.

Pauline Newbery

If a man cannot get an erection, boil the herb agrimony in milk and let him drink much.
old *Book of Shadows*, via *Patricia Crowther*

ALDER, COMMON *Alnus glutinosa*

Alder is good for inflammation of the feet: bathe them in a warm decoction of the leaves.
Rheumatism can also be relieved by applying hot leaves to the affected parts.

Patricia Crowther

ANEMONE, WOOD *Anemone nemorosa*

As a cure for all disease, pick the first anemone

alfalfa
Buffalo Herb

you see in the year, and say, 'Anemone I greet ye
in the name of the Great Goddess'. Wrap the
flower in fair linen or parchment, and keep
hidden till needed. Kiss your thumb, held
between your two fingers in honour of the
Goddess, before and after doing this. Give to the
sick person, saying, 'I give you this year's
anemone to cure you in the name of the Great
Goddess'. You kiss your thumb and make the
sick person do likewise.

old *Book of Shadows*, via *Patricia Crowther*

ANGELICA *Angelica archangelica*

Angelica is perhaps best known today for its candied stems,
much used by cooks. However, it has long been valued for
its medicinal properties, foremost among them its ability to
help the digestion. It is a useful appetiser, and may also be
taken to ease indigestion, flatulence and colic.

The parts of the herb used are the roots and leaves.
Roots should be dug in the autumn of the first year of
growth, when it is least likely to have been damaged by
pests. Thick roots may need slicing lengthways to aid drying.

Preparation and dosage: make an infusion by pouring
600 ml/1 pt/2½ cups of boiling water on to 25 g/1 oz bruised
root; take 30 ml/2 tbsp 3–4 times a day. In small doses, it is
a tonic; if larger amounts are drunk it has a depressant
effect.

> The stalks and roots are the parts used. Angelica
> is useful in treating digestive problems and also
> stimulates the appetite. Eat the roots candied or
> soaked in vinegar to combat infections. As
> protective talismans against the 'black arts', keep
> angelica leaves on the person and/or place them
> around the house.
>
> *Pauline Newbery*

ANISE *Pimpinella anisum*

This spice has been employed for many years, principally in

Europe, to flavour such foods as bread, cakes, salads and soups. It is also an ingredient of the popular liquor anisette. Apart from being a refreshing drink, it has a beneficial effect on the bronchial tubes, affording relief to sufferers from bronchitis and asthma. The part of the herb used is the fruit (often mistakenly called the seed), from which the oil is extracted. This is good for gastric problems such as flatulence, colic and sluggish digestion; the remedy is a dose of essence of aniseed in a glass of hot water.

Preparation and dosage: aniseed tea is easily prepared. Pour 300 ml/¹/₂ pt/1¹/₄ cups of boiling water on to 10 ml/2 tsp of bruised fruit. Drink cold, sweetened if desired. This is beneficial for children suffering from catarrh, the dose here being 5–15ml/1–3 tsp taken frequently. For adults suffering from nervousness and insomnia, larger amounts make an effective sedative.

APPLE *Pyrus malus*

The apple is regarded by witches as a sacred fruit. If you cut an apple across, at the point where the seeds rest, you will see that the pips form the pattern of a five-pointed star or pentagram. This symbol is traditionally associated with witchcraft.

The apple is a very good all-round health food and it is particularly beneficial for curing constipation. Apples also keep the teeth clean and freshen the mouth. Always try to obtain organically grown apples that have not been sprayed with toxic pesticide, or grow your own, if you have space for a tree or two in your garden.

> To firm facial tissues, pulp an apple and apply
> over the face or use the juice. Leave for a couple
> of minutes and rinse off.
>
> *Sylvia Guyatt*

BALM *Melissa officinalis*

This herb, often called sweet balm or lemon balm because of the fragrant lemon scent released when it is bruised, is useful to those suffering from digestive disorders such as wind, gynaecological and nervous problems.

To make balm tea: pour 600 ml/1 pt/2½ cups of boiling water on to 25 g/1 oz fresh herbs or 20 ml/1 heaped tbsp dried herb (leaves and flowers), infuse until cool, then strain and consume freely. With the addition of sugar and a few slices of lemon, it makes a pleasant summer drink. A few sprigs of balm bestow a palatable flavour to most cups.

Balm leaves, applied externally, make excellent dressings for wounds, as they give off ozone, which protects against infection, and then dry on the sores, sealing them against airborne germs.

Balm is also a good treatment for influenza.
Preparation and dosage: make a tea of 25 g/1 oz of the fresh leaves or 20 ml/1 heaped tbsp of dried leaves to 600 ml/1 pt/2½ cups of boiling water. Infuse for 15 minutes, then strain. Drink 1–2 cups hot. A cup at bedtime will help you sleep well.

Sylvia Guyatt

BANANA *Musa paradisiaca*

Plantain fruit, more commonly known as bananas, are said to cure impotence and increase fertility. Eat one or two a day, at the end of a meal.

BASIL, SWEET *Ocymum basilium*

Sweet basil is popular with cooks in France, who employ it to impart an appetising flavour to soups, stews and sauces. The leaves have a scent much like cloves. There is a strange superstition associated with sweet basil: it was said that scorpions were drawn to the plant, and liked to live under the containers in which it grew.

Medicinally, it has anti-inflammatory powers and it is also a tonic; the flowers and leaves are used as an infusion. Additionally, it possesses disinfectant properties. In India the plant – sacred to Hindus – is also highly valued in the home as a protection against malaria.

Sprinkled on the body, it is said to posses the magical

ability to bring riches.

Useful in poultice in drawing out poison

Basil is beneficial for headaches, stomach cramps, vomiting and gastro-enteritis.

Preparation and dosage: make an infusion by steeping 15 ml/1 tbsp of the fresh herb or 5 ml/1 tsp of the dried herb in 120 ml/4 fl oz/ 1/2 cup of hot water. Take 1–1 1/2 cups a day, a mouthful at a time.

Kim Tracey

Basil leaves act as a fly repellent. A pot of basil set on a windowsill or table will help to reduce the number of flies in a room. Water well from the bottom so the plant produces plenty of scent.

Linda Bruce

BEANS (kidney, snap, string, etc.)

Beans are said to lower the blood sugar level in mild diabetes.

Preparation and dosage: make a decoction of 30 ml/2 tbsp of the pods and beans (chopped into small pieces) in 1.2 litres/2 pts/5 cups of water. Boil for 3 hours. Take 600–900 ml/ 1–1 1/2 pts/2 1/2–3 3/4 cups a day.

Kim Tracey

BETONY, WOOD see Mint *Betonica officinalis*

For loss of strength, steep betony in wine and honey and drink until the tiredness goes.

old *Book of Shadows,* via *Patricia Crowther*

For toothache, boil betony in wine till there be only one-third left of the liquid. Hold this in the mouth a long time and keep warm in bed and the pain will ease.

old *Book of Shadows,* via *Patricia Crowther*

BIRCH, SILVER *Betula pendula*

Birch sap is superb for skin eruptions and in

early spring can be used to sweeten your tea.

Chris Bray

BLACKBERRY *Rubus fructicosus*

One of the most familiar sights in the British countryside is this rambler bush which is found in the hedgerow or on uncultivated land. Bramble leaves, applied externally, help to heal burns and scalds. This may account for the fact that the bush is called scaldhead in some parts of Britain. Alternative theories are that it is so named because an eruption called scaldhead appears on children who eat too much of the fruit, or because the leaves and berries of the bramble have a beneficial effect on this scalp disorder.

> For the treatment of cystitis, crush dried blackberry leaves – a good handful - and add to 1 litre/1³/₄ pts/4¹/₄ cups of water. Boil for 5 minutes, then infuse for 10 minutes. Strain and drink. Take 2–3 cups a day between meals.
>
> *Sylvia Guyatt*

> Blackberry cordial is an excellent remedy for winter colds and sore throats; 15 ml/1 tbsp in a glass of hot water makes a comforting bedtime drink. **To make:** collect 1.2 litres/2 pts/5 cups of ripe blackberries, place them in an earthenware jar and pour over 600 ml/1 pt/2¹/₂ cups of white vinegar. Let the mixture stand for 7–8 days, stirring occasionally to extract the juice. Strain and place the liquid in an enamel saucepan with 450 g/1 lb/2 cups of loaf sugar and 225 g/8 oz/³/₄ cup of honey. Bring to the boil, then remove from the heat and allow to cool. Bottle and cork and keep in a dark place.
>
> *Linda Bruce*

BORAGE *Borago officinalis*

> An infusion of borage is good as an eye wash to alleviate inflammation and redness.
>
> *Sylvia Guyatt*

BREAD MOULD

Bread mould has been used by witches for centuries as an antiseptic for serious or septic wounds. We now know, of course, that it is a close relative of penicillin, so this is another case in which scientific analysis has confirmed ancient practices.

Chris Bray

BRYONY (SNAKE GRAPES) *Bryonia dioica*

Warning!
This herb is poisonous in large doses. Do not experiment with this recipe.

The juice obtained by boiling a handful of leaves in 600 ml/1 pt/2½ cups of water, when mixed with an equal amount of white wine, helps to heal and strengthen broken bones. Drink a small wineglassful of the mixture every day for a week.

Pauline Newbery

BURDOCK *Arctium lappa*

This member of the thistle family, which grows abundantly in hedges and on waste ground, is much valued as a remedy for skin diseases, especially eczema and boils. A mild laxative may be obtained by eating the stalks as a vegetable. Gather them before the flower is open, strip off the rind and boil. Alternatively they may be eaten raw in salad, with an oil and vinegar dressing.

An infusion or decoction of burdock seeds is said to possess diuretic properties in cases of water retention and kidney disease. In the latter case, it is recommended that the remedy be drunk several times a day, before meals. The leaves of this herb, applied externally as a poultice, are most effective in reducing bruises, gouty swellings and other inflamed skin surfaces.

Preparation and dosage: a decoction is made from the root and seeds of the plant, 25 g/1 oz to 900 ml/1½ pts/ 3¾ cups of water, reduced to 600 ml/1 pt/2½ cups. Take one wineglassful 3–4 times a day. This preparation is also beneficial as a lotion for psoriasis.

A tea made from burdock leaves will purify the blood.

Cylch Cyhiraeth

BUTTERCUP *Ranunculus bulbosus*

Buttercup ointment is very good for all skin problems. To make it, put 225 g/8 oz/1 cup of pure Vaseline into a pan with as many buttercup flowers (without the stalks) as can be pressed into it. Simmer for 45 minutes, not allowing the mixture to boil. While still hot, strain through a muslin-lined sieve into sterile screw-top jars (see instructions on sterilising containers on p10). It is ready to use when it has cooled.

Linda Bruce

CARROT *Daucus carota*

Raw and grated and mixed with lemon juice, carrot removes blotches on the skin and helps combat wrinkles! Add enough lemon juice to make a paste that will stay on your face and not slide down. Place the mixture on the offending parts of the skin and leave for at least 30 minutes.

Patricia Crowther

Carrots are said to be effective in curing impotence and increasing libido.

CARAWAY see Garlic *Carum carvi*

CATMINT *Nepeta cataria*

 This herb, also known as catnip, is a member of the mint family. It is much loved by cats who adore toy cloth mice that have been stuffed with it. Either growing or dried, catmint will intoxicate and keep a new cat from straying from home.

Pauline Newbery

For the treatment of bruises, put 25 g/1 oz fresh catmint or 20 ml/1 heaped tbsp of dried catmint into 600 ml/1 pt/2½ cups water. Put into a muslin bag and boil. Allow the liquid to cool and drink small measures (a liqueur glass size) 3 times a day. The liquid may also be dabbed on to the affected area, so long as the skin is not broken.

Pauline Newbery

Catmint will help those suffering from stomach upsets, flatulence, acidity and sleeplessness.

Preparation and dosage: pour 1 cup of water that has just boiled on to 5 ml/1 tsp of the herb, but take care that the water is not still on the boil. Drink 1–2 cups a day.

Kim Tracey

CELANDINE, GREATER *Chelidonium majus*

This plant, which produces bright yellow flowers, is a member of the poppy family. The fresh orange-yellow juice, when applied externally to warts, should remove them in one week.

Celandine can be used to relieve jaundice. Take a wineglassful of the juice (strained) before each meal.

One of the magical uses of the herb is in the form of an amulet, worn to protect the wearer against imprisonment.

Pauline Newbery

CHAMOMILE, COMMON *Anthemis nobilis*

The common chamomile releases a distinct scent of apples, especially when stepped on. It may be confused with the German chamomile (sometimes called the wild chamomile), but not so readily mistaken for the stinking chamomile which – as its name implies – possesses a most unattractive odour.

In bygone times chamomile was called the 'plants' physician' because if it was placed in the garden near another plant that was ailing, the sickly neighbour would nearly always recover.

To make chamomile tea: this well-known tea is an infusion of 25 g/1 oz of chamomile flowers in 600 ml/1 pt/ 2½ cups of boiling water; allow it to stand for at least 10 minutes with the lid on the pot so the goodness does not evaporate away, then strain. This is a most effective sedative that despite its bitter taster is harmless to all. It is said to be a sure-fire remedy for nightmares, and will assist in an attack of delirium tremens. Chamomile tea is also good for digestive problems such as loss of appetite, especially in the elderly, heartburn, indigestion, flatulence, colic and a sluggish intestine. A strong, warm infusion of the herb is a good emetic (induces vomiting).

Old herbals say that chamomile flowers possess antiseptic properties 120 times more powerful than sea water. Sadly, no one could today recommend the latter as an antiseptic because of marine pollution, but there is nothing wrong with chamomile flowers, provided they have been gathered in an area free from contamination.

Used externally, an infusion of chamomile makes a good wash for inflamed skin, wounds, open sores and irritated eyes.

> Use an infusion of chamomile as a lotion and apply to the affected parts when suffering from earache, neuralgia or swollen glands.
>
> *Sylvia Guyatt*

CHICKWEED *Stellaria media*

> To treat skin wounds and ulcers, gather enough chickweed to cover the wound and pour boiling water over it. Then bind it over the wound.
>
> *Linda Bruce*

CIDER VINEGAR

> If you are doubtful about the freshness of food you are about to consume, take 10 ml/2 tsp of cider vinegar neat, before or after the meal, and

food poisoning will never be a problem. Cider vinegar could therefore be the answer when visiting countries that have suspect standards of food preparation.

Cider vinegar, diluted to taste and taken 3 times a day, helps prevent arthritis and hardening of the arteries. It also keeps the body pure by helping it to rid itself of toxins.

Take 60 ml/4 tsp of cider vinegar in a glass of cold water to help a hangover.

All from Jackie James

CLEAVERS   *Galium aparine*

> **Warning!**
> *This is a powerful diuretic which would upset diabetics. Not recommended for use by them.*

An infusion of cleavers – also known as goosegrass – helps you lose weight.

Used as a hair rinse, an infusion of goosegrass is effective against dandruff.

Both from Cylch Cyhiraeth

COMFREY   *Symphytum officinale*

Boneset or knitbone – country names for comfrey – was often used as a poultice, but the mucilage (sticky substance) in the root enabled it to be soaked and pulverised into a pliable mass, which after application dried smooth, tight and firm on broken bones. It is much better than plaster of Paris, for you simply soak it again to get it off and you can even eat it. Boneset root was used in the same way to make effigies and mould patterns.

Chris Bray

For ageing skin, bruise comfrey leaves and rub on to the skin as a face wash. They have an astringent effect. Wash off the face after a few minutes with warm water.

Sylvia Guyatt

CUCUMBER *Cucumis sativa*

The seeds of this ancient plant, known to have been cultivated in the East 3,000 years ago, are believed to increase fertility.

CYCLAMEN, IVY-LEAVED *Cyclamen hederaefolium*

The tuberous roots of this plant, occasionally found in the wilds of Kent and Sussex in England, are the parts used, and should be dug up when the cyclamen is flowering. In times past these roots were made into small cakes and baked; it was believed that those who ate them would fall in love. Today the roots are used to increase a woman's chances of conceiving a child. Chop up the cleaned roots and add to the cake mixture, as you would currants or glacé cherries.

DAISY (COMMON LAWN) *Bellis perennis*

This is a tonic, a remedy for digestive problems and a gentle laxative. Make an ointment with the fresh flowers to help heal swellings and burns. The tea is good for catarrh, colic and bladder ailments.

Preparation and dosage: make an infusion of 5 ml/1 tsp of fresh flowers to 250 ml/8 fl oz/ 1 cup of water. Steep for 5 minutes, strain and drink warm, 1 cup a day.

Sylvia Guyatt

DANDELION *Taraxacum officinale*

Dandelion may be taken as a diuretic and for stomach disorders. This herb encourages the formation of bile and removes excess water from the body resulting from liver problems. It is recommended for dyspepsia, constipation, fever, sleeplessness, hypochondria, chronic rheumatism, gout and stiffness of the joints.

Preparation and dosage: the complete plant may be used before flowering, the leaves used during flowering and the root alone in the autumn. Make an infusion of 10 ml/2 tsp of the plant or root in 250 ml/8 fl oz/1 cup of boiling water. Take ½–1 cup a day, lukewarm or cold.

Kim Tracey

Dandelion juice will remove warts.

Cylch Cyhiraeth

DOCK, ROUND-LEAVED *Rumex obtusifolius*

Dock leaves rubbed on to nettle stings will ease the pain. They are also useful for minor bruises.

Jackie James

ELDER *Sambucus nigra*

Elder is traditionally associated with death (it was used in ancient burial rites in this country) and with witches (witches and spirits were said to reside in it).

Medicinally, wine made from the black berries is said to be an aid to pain in childbirth.

Boil the bark in a salt-water solution to make a lotion to bathe painful feet.

Boil the flowers in borage water and drink a glassful morning and evening for a good skin and to keep your youthful looks. You can make the drink as strong or as weak as you like – elderflowers can do no harm. As a rough guide, use the usual herbal tea dose of 25 g/1 oz of fresh herbs or 20 ml/1 heaped tbsp of dried herbs to 600 ml/1 pt/2½ cups of water.

Pauline Newbery

Elderflower eye wash is beneficial for tired and dull eyes. It is also good for softening the skin; use on a cotton wool pad. Keep the solution in the fridge when not in use; it stays fresher longer that way.

Preparation and use: pour 600 ml/1 pt/
2½ cups of boiling water over 5 or 6 fresh or
dried flowers. Leave to infuse for 10 minutes.
Strain through a coffee filter paper. Cool and use
in an eye bath.

Sylvia Guyatt

Elderberry wine is good for stomach disorders
and for reducing inflammation.

Cylch Cyhiraeth

The juice of elderberries makes an effective hair
dye; gypsies use it for this purpose. Alternatively,
crush the fruit and apply to wet hair. Leave for
20–30 minutes and rinse off.

Sylvia Guyatt

For centuries elderberries have had the reputation of helping those suffering from rheumatism. The berries may be
made into a wine which is also well known for its ability to
ease the miseries of colds and influenza, as it promotes perspiration; drink it hot, with a little cinnamon added, if
desired. Elderberry wine is also said to ease asthma.

There are a multitude of recipes for elderberry wine.
Here is one that appeared in a book published in 1825:

'To make 2 gallons of wine, pick 1 gallon of
elderberries and a quart of damsons or sloes and
boil them together in 6 quarts of water for half
an hour, breaking up the fruit with a stick. Run
off the liquor and squeeze the pulp through a
sieve or straining cloth. Boil the liquor up again
with 6 lb of coarse sugar, 2 oz of ginger, 2 oz of
bruised allspice and 1 oz of hops (the spices to
be tied up in a piece of muslin). Let this boil for
half an hour, then pour it off. When quite cool,
add a cupful of yeast and cover it up to work.
After 2 days skim off the yeast and put the wine
into a barrel. When it ceases to hiss, which will
be after about a fortnight, paste a piece of stiff
brown paper over the bung-hole. The wine will

be fit for use in about 8 weeks, and may be kept for 8 years.'

Another very old way of using elderberries is to make a 'rob', which is similar to a syrup. This, too, is most useful in cases of colds, coughs and bronchitis. Elderberry rob is made by simmering 2.25 kg/5 lb of crushed ripe berries with 450 g/1 lb/2 cups of loaf sugar until the mixture reduces to the consistency of honey. Take 15–30 ml/1–2 tbsp diluted in a tumbler of hot water, at night. The rob is particularly useful because it can be bottled and kept for the winter.

Elderberries are also believed to cure warts.

> Elderflower ointment makes a good salve. To prepare, melt 450 g/1 lb/2 cups clarified lard in a pan and add 4.5 litres/1 gallon of elderflower heads. Boil until they are pulped, then strain and add a few drops of turpentine. Pour into sterile screw-top jars and leave to set.
>
> *Linda Bruce*

ELDER LEAVES see Onion

ELECAMPANE *Inula helenium*

Mediterranean people may have used garlic as an antiseptic for disease, but healers in this country traditionally use the root of elecampane, which contains inulin. Elecampane root is particularly useful for the alleviation of bronchial diseases.

Chris Bray

This herb has been used medicinally for thousands of years. The Romans believed that 'Elecampane will the spirits sustain', and also believed that it aided digestion. Later on monks used it in the treatment of lung complaints. The tall plants with their bright yellow flowers and huge leaves may still be found growing near old monasteries.

The part employed is the root, which should be dug up in the autumn when a plant is 2–3 years old; if older it will be too woody. A decoction of this, either taken internally or applied as a wash, is a highly effective remedy for itching skin or skin diseases such as eczema and simple herpes.

As mentioned above, a decoction of the herb has long been given for pulmonary disease. It is valuable to sufferers of asthma.

EUCALYPTUS *Eucalyptus globulus*

> **Warning!**
> *Eucalyptus oil is said to increase heart action, so it is not recommended for use by those with heart trouble.*

Oil from the leaves of the eucalyptus tree, which has the strange property of drying out the ground around its roots (useful, for example, in marshy areas of hot countries where the malaria mosquito flourishes), is a powerful antiseptic.

Mixed with water, it is used as a gargle for sore throats that are associated with colds. The oil may also be applied freely to the skin around the throat of sufferers from dry coughs.

Applied externally, eucalyptus oil is most effective as a cleanser of infected skin in both people and animals; in the past it was used to treat dogs with distemper, for example.

FENNEL *Foeniculum vulgare*

 This plant is traditionally used in charms and brews to ward off evil. Medicinally, boiled in equal parts of milk and water, it cures hiccoughs and eases indigestion. When the leaves and seeds are boiled together, it is an aid to slimming. Fennel juice placed directly on to the tongue cures vomiting.

Pauline Newbery

FEVERFEW *Chrysanthemum parthenium*

> **Warning!**
> *Feverfew is an emmenagogue (induces menstruation), so it is to be avoided by those who think they may be pregnant.*

Use this plant to treat colic, flatulence, indigestion and colds. A cold extract of feverfew has a tonic effect.

Preparation and dosage: make an infusion of 25 g/1 oz of fresh herb or 20 ml/1 heaped tbsp of dried herb in 600 ml/1 pt/2½ cups water. Take 1–2 cups a day. You could take one dose (15 ml/1 tbsp) each hour.

Kim Tracey

Feverfew helps migraine. It has a bitter taste, so a few leaves eaten as the filling in a sandwich is the best way to take this herb.

Patricia Crowther

FOXGLOVE *Digitalis purpurea*

> **Warning!**
> *Digitalis is dangerous and should only be taken under medical supervision.*

The handsome foxglove is a welcome sight in woods and lanes, but should be treated with great care as it is highly poisonous. Even touching it with bare skin can cause a rash, nausea and headache.

The foxglove, otherwise known as digitalis, contains four powerful drugs employed mainly to help those with heart diseases; three of the four are cardiac stimulants. These drugs are extracted from its leaves.

It has also been used in the treatment of such disorders as delirium tremens, epilepsy and acute mania, because of the narcotic and sedative properties it also possesses.

FUMITORY *Fumaria officinalis*

Used primarily for problems connected with the liver and gall bladder. Large doses of fumitory act as a laxative and diuretic.

Preparation and dosage: use the dried flowers and leaves. Make an infusion of 7.5 ml/ 1 heaped tsp of the herb to 250 ml/8 fl oz/1 cup of hot water. Let this cool and take a cold wineglassful every 4 hours. As an alternative, make a cold extract by steeping 5 ml/1 tsp of the herb in 120 ml/4 fl oz/¹/₂ cup of cold water for 8–10 hours. Take 2.5–5 ml/¹/₂–1 tsp at a time.

Kim Tracey

GARLIC *Allium sativum* See also Heather

This plant is so ancient that it is not possible to establish its country of origin. It has been grown in England since before 1540. Garlic has been advocated over the years for a multitude of complaints; in fact, one of its old country names was 'poor man's treacle', 'treacle' being a corruption of the Greek word *theriac* meaning 'heal-all'.

Today the herb is popular with cooks – for its taste, its ability to keep the stomach lining healthy and as an aid to digestion. The part employed is the bulb.

It is also valued as an antiseptic. During the First World War, wounds were protected from possible infection by being dressed with pieces of sphagnum moss soaked in a mixture of garlic juice and water. The lives of many thousands of soldiers were said to have been saved in this way. Diluted garlic juice may also be applied externally as a lotion or ointment.

Since ancient times, garlic has traditionally been kept at hand as a defence against demons and the 'black arts'.

For dental abscesses, crush a garlic clove and apply to the cavity. It kills the pain, as do caraway seeds.

Sylvia Guyatt

GINGER *Zingiber officinale*

For travel sickness, chew a ginger root or add 5 ml/1 tsp of ground ginger to a glass of hot milk.

Linda Bruce

GOAT'S RUE *Galega officinalis*

> **Warning!**
> *A poison if taken in excessive doses. It is also an emmena-gogue (induces menstruation), so should be avoided by anyone who thinks they may be pregnant.*

This pea-like plant is beneficial to those suffering from rheumatism. The leaves and flowering tops of the herb are used to make an infusion. Goat's rue, which may be so called because of the unpleasant odour released when the plant is bruised, is also a diaphoretic (induces perspiration). Do not take after meals because it has emetic tendencies. When given to cows, it increases their milk yield dramatically.

GOLDEN ROD *Solidago virgaurea*

> **Warning!**
> *Helpful for amenorrhoea (absence of menstruation), so is contra-indicated in pregnancy.*

Warm, sweet golden rod tea has diaphoretic (perspiration-inducing) properties. Drunk cold it stimulates the system and eases flatulence.

Preparation and dosage: steep 5 ml/1 tsp of dried leaves or 15 ml/1 tbsp of fresh leaves in 250 ml/8 fl oz/1 cup of warm water. Take 1–2 cups a day, warm or cold, according to your need.

Kim Tracey

GROUNDSEL *Senecio vulgaris*

For persistent coughs, take a bowlful of groundsel flowers and leaves and wash well, discarding the stalks. Add as much water as you have herb. Place in a saucepan, bring to the boil, then simmer until the liquid has reduced to half the original quantity. Strain and add the juice of 2 lemons and 10 ml/2 tsp of honey. Take 10 ml/ 2 tsp every time you start to cough. This very old recipe can work like magic in just a few days. If the cough persists, however, consult your doctor.

Linda Bruce

HAWTHORN *Crataegus oxyacantha*

> **Warning!**
> *Not to be used by those with heart conditions unless under the care of a qualified herbalist.*

A decoction of the flowers of the hawthorn, often called may, will draw out any splinter or thorn.

Chris Bray

Hawthorn (haws and flowers) is a strong tonic and sedative, good for lack of energy and insomnia. It is said to be able to help normalise blood pressure, whether high or low.

Preparation and dosage: use 10 ml/2 tsp of the flowers to 250 ml/8 fl oz/1 cup of boiling water. Cover and infuse 5–10 minutes. Strain and drink hot, slowly, in small sips, ¹/₂–1 cup daily before or between meals.

Sylvia Guyatt

HEATHER *Calluna vulgaris*

Heather flowers will help with cystitis.

Preparation and dosage: add 3 handfuls of the fresh flowers or 1 handful of the dried flowers to 1 litre/1³/₄ pts/4¹/₄ cups of boiling water. Boil for 5 minutes, then cool and strain. Drink 2–3 cups daily until cured. You can also use garlic, parsley and pearl barley teas for cystitis.

Sylvia Guyatt

HELLEBORE, BLACK *Helleborus niger*

> **Warning!**
> *Hellebore should only be used under expert supervision.*

This poisonous herb is the pretty plant known as the Christmas rose, that blooms in midwinter. The drug contained in its root is a drastic purgative (particularly indicated where intestinal worms are concerned) and emmenagogue (induces or increases menstrual flow). It is also a powerful narcotic, and was formally used in cases of nervous disorders and hysteria. Contact with the plant may cause a violent skin reaction.

HEMLOCK *Conium maculatum*

> **Warning!**
> *A strong poison, only to be used under expert supervision.*

Amputations were once performed with a brew made from hemlock, henbane and belladonna leaves. Judging the effects of such powerful drugs was obviously an important skill and witches used to test their brews on small animals to calculate their power. A cup of this mixture would be given to render the patient unconscious and a 'soporific sponge' (a sponge soaked in the fluid) was kept pressed to the mouth to deepen the sleep when necessary during the operation.

Chris Bray

To aid meditation, astral projection and clear the head of distractions, place some dried hemlock in a white cotton bag, soak the bag in warm olive oil and rub it on the forehead. Such a bag is also used to rub on magic tools to cleanse them psychically. Wiccans believe that objects 'carry' information about their owners or what they have been used for in the past. When psychics use psychometry to glean information about a person or the history of an object, they are picking up on this life. By cleaning a magic tool with hemlock, Wiccans believe they are removing unwanted 'messages' absorbed by the object.

Cylch Cyhiraeth

HENBANE *Hyoscyamus niger*

> **Warning!**
> *This herb should only be used under expert supervision.*

Henbane is poisonous in *all* its parts, but as the plant has a most unpleasant smell – and taste – it is unlikely to be mistaken for a vegetable. Today it is much in demand, being the source of the drugs hyoscyamine, atropine and scopolamine, so much used by conventional doctors. These are abstracted from the leaves, flowering tops and branches of the plant. In times past henbane was used as a sedative and narcotic, as it combines the two therapeutic actions of relaxing spasms of the involuntary muscles and relieving pain, and was valuable in easing the suffering of those with such ailments as irritable bladder, hysteria and severe nervous irritability. A linament that contained henbane was also effective in relieving rheumatism.

Witches used to pull out teeth painlessly by making those afflicted with toothache inhale the vapours from henbane seeds which were sintered (converted into cinders) on a hotplate. The herb seeds were roughly crushed, placed in a metal dish and heated until they began to burn and give off a vapour. General mouth anaesthesia occurred along with a 'twilight' sleep which made the patient co-operative.

Chris Bray

HOLLY *Ilex aquifolium*

For a tight chest, boil holly bark in goat's milk and sip while warm. Fast for a day. (Early

Anglo-Saxon remedy). Do not eat the berries, which will make you violently sick. If chest discomfort or pain persists, consult your doctor.

Linда Bruce

HOLLY, SEA *Eryngium maritinum*

> **Warning!**
> *A stimulant when taken internally, so not to be used by those with heart problems.*

For bites and stings of all sorts, take sea holly, crush into a plaster and lay on the wound. If necessary, lance the wound.

old *Book of Shadows* via *Patricia Crowther*

HONEY

Honey in hot water at bedtime induces sleep.

Cover burns immediately with honey; they will heal magically.

Treat cuts by washing under running water, then pour on honey and bind with a clean bandage. Most cuts will heal overnight.

For nappy rash, wash skin, cover with honey and put on a clean nappy. The rash will be healed by the next change.

Take 30 ml/2 tbsp of honey and 10 ml/2 tsp of cider vinegar in a tumbler of hot water first thing every day. It purifies the inner person (i.e. removes toxins from the body), gives energy and prevents most minor illnesses. Toxins are ingested by drinking too much alcohol, coffee or tea, or eating food containing additives. Take the same dosage 3 times daily to cure colds and 'flu.

All from Jackie James

HORSETAILS *Equisetum* class of plants

> ***Warning!***
> *An emmenagogue (induces menstruation), so do not take if pregnant.*

Horsetails are an antiseptic. Only the barren stems which appear after the fruiting stems have died down are used. Sever them just above the root. The herb is most effective applied when fresh, but it is also valuable dried.

Cylch Cyhiraeth

HOUSELEEK *Sempervivum tectorum*

For corns and hard skin on feet, apply a poultice made from the pulpy inner part of houseleek leaves. If taken internally, in large doses, it is an emetic, so use with care.

To ease insect bites, rub them with the pulpy inner part of houseleek leaves.

The houseleek has large rosettes of fleshy leaves and big clusters of dark pink flowers, said to resemble Jupiter's beard (one of the plant's old nicknames). Houseleeks were often grown on cottage roofs, in Britain and Europe, because it was believed they protected the dwelling from fire and lightning. Many superstitions are still centred on the plant.

Both from Cylch Cyhiraeth

HYACINTH, WILD *Hyacinthus nonscriptus*

This plant, better known as the bluebell, is said to ease the process of childbirth. When fresh, the bulbs are poisonous; dry and pound them to a powder, and sprinkle on food to eat as a medicine. Wild hyacinth in doses not exceeding 3 grains (1 grain = 0.065 g) is a good remedy for leucorrhoea (mucous vaginal discharge).

The sticky juice found particularly in the bulb, is a starch substitute and was used for stiffening ruffs in the past.

HYSSOP *Hyssopus officinalis*

> **Warning!**
> *A stimulant, so not to be used on those with heart problems.*

Hyssop is an effective expectorant (promotes the expulsion of mucus from the respiratory passages). It is also useful in treating poor digestion, lung diseases, cold-induced coughs and nose and throat infections. A decoction of this herb will help to relieve inflammation.

Preparation and dosage: steep 5 ml/1 tsp of hyssop in 120 ml/4 fl oz/½ cup of hot water. Take ½–1½ cups a day, a mouthful at at time. Sweeten with honey if desired.

Kim Tracey

LAUREL (BAY) *Laurus nobilis*

> **Warning!**
> *Not to be used by pregnant women. Care should be taken as the berries have in the past been used to procure abortion.*

The leaves of the true laurel or sweet bay tree are deservedly popular with cooks as they add flavour to a dish and aid digestion. A tea made from the leaves and berries is said to be a good tonic and an effective emmenagogue (induces or increases menstrual flow).

Oil of bay, extracted from the berries, is beneficial when rubbed on to sprains, bruises, etc. Massage in gently over rheumaticky joints.

Added to bath water, the oil has a pleasantly relaxing effect and possesses deodorising properties.

LEMON see Nettle *Citrus limonum*

LETTUCE, WILD *Lactuca virosa*

The juice of wild lettuce, sometimes called green endive, has a narcotic effect. Rub it on to the forehead to relax and encourage sleep. The juice of garden lettuce, *Lactuca sativa,* also acts in this way, but with less potency.

MALLOW, BLUE *Malva sylvestris*

This tall, tough plant with pretty dark mauve flowers is commonly found in fields, hedgerows and on waste ground. A poultice made from its leaves and flowers is good for inflammation and an infusion (of the same parts of the plant) is a remedy for coughs and colds. A cool infusion is also beneficial as a lotion for swollen eyelids.

A decoction of the herb added to bath water is believed to have a 'gentling' effect on the personality, rubbing off the 'rough corners' in both men and women.

MALLOW, MARSH *Althaea officinalis*

Often the simplest remedies are the best and most effective. One woman who was in terrible pain with a stomach ulcer and who had tried any number of drugs and specialists, found relief drinking a tisane of marsh mallow leaves every other day or so. Always consult your doctor in cases of severe stomach pain.

Chris Bray

MANDRAKE *Atropa mandragora*

> **Warning!**
> *The root is poisonous and experiments involving its use should not be embarked upon without expert supervision.*

The mandrake plant, about which so many legends have been woven, has a long brown root reminiscent of a parsnip and large dark tongue-like leaves which, when fully grown, lie flat on the ground and exude an unpleasant smell. Its flowers are similar to a whitish primrose.

The fresh root is the part that has medicinal value, in particular for hay fever, asthma and coughs. It has a narcotic effect and it is also a powerful emetic (induces vomiting) and purgative. The leaves are perfectly harmless.

A whole root which resembles the human form has long
been regarded as a potent magic charm. Carry it when help
is needed in any undertaking and it will bring success; touch
it in moments of stress to bring tranquility; keep it close for
fertility.

MARIGOLD *Calendula officinalis*

Marigold is considered one of the best herbs for
treating cuts, sores and minor burns.

To make an ointment: melt 200 g/7 oz/1 cup
of petroleum jelly over a low heat and add
60 g/2½ oz of freshly picked marigold flowers.
Bring the mixture to the boil and let it simmer
very gently for about 10 minutes, stirring
frequently. Sieve it through a piece of fine gauze,
pressing all the liquid from the flowers. Pour the
salve into a sterile screw-top jar and seal when
cool.

Kim Tracey

Rub the deep orange flowers of marigold on
wasp or bee stings to relieve pain and
inflammation.

For cuts and sores, bruise marigold leaves and
apply. They are antiseptic.

Both from Sylvia Guyatt

MARJORAM, WILD *Origanum vulgare*

> **Warning!**
> *Taken internally, this is an emmenagogue, so it should not
> be taken by pregnant women.*

This aromatic herb is a perennial. The flowery tops of the
plant are used to make a warm infusion beneficial to sufferers from digestive problems such as dyspepsia and colic.
The preparation is also a remedy for headaches.

Used externally, a hot fomentation of marjoram leaves
and tops will bring relief from rheumatism, painful swellings
and cramps.

Boil marjoram in water for 20 minutes and use as a poultice for arthritis.

Sylvia Guyatt

MEADOWSWEET *Spiraea ulmaria*

This herb can be used for gout, kidney ailments, bladder problems, respiratory conditions, arthritis, fever, water retention, headaches and influenza.

Preparation and dosage: make an infusion of 30 ml/2 tbsp of fresh meadowsweet added to 250 ml/8 fl oz/1 cup of hot water. Drink a cup a day. If you wish to make a larger quantity, the usual dose is 75 g/3 oz of fresh herb or 25 g/1 oz of dried herb to 600 ml/1 pt/2½ cups of water. The herb is collected in July, when it is flowering.

Kim Tracey

MINT (PEPPERMINT) *Mentha piperita*

> **Warning!**
> *Those suffering from heart trouble should only take this as prescribed by a qualified herbalist.*

Oil of peppermint, whose chief constituent is menthol, is renowned for its powers to relieve pain in the digestive system. A glass of peppermint oil in hot water (or 1–2 drops of the oil on a lump of sugar) does wonders for such problems as indigestion, flatulence and colic. It will also benefit those suffering from sickness and nausea (including sea sickness). For nervous disorders, an infusion of peppermint (using the leaves and flowery tops) is most helpful; adding an equal amount of wood betony (the whole herb, collected in July if possible) is said to increase the efficacy of this remedy. The herb is also reputed to make a good tonic.

MISTLETOE *Viscum album*

> **Warning!**
> *The white berries should never be used for medicinal purposes, as they are poisonous.*

This evergreen parasitic plant can be found growing on the branches of deciduous trees such as apple, ash, hawthorn, lime and oak. It has a strong occult tradition, being particularly used in love spells. Mistletoe is a relaxant which soothes the nervous system. However, advice from a trained herbalist should always be sought before using this plant because large doses can be dangerous.

MOSS

Moss stops bleeding. It is particularly useful if an accident occurs in a park or remote country place where there is no chemist or medical facility. Before application, however, make sure that no earth or dog or other animal faeces are attached to the moss. It must be quite clean.

Jackie James

MOTHERWORT *Leonurus cardiaca*

> **Warning!**
> *Not to be used by pregnant women or those with heart trouble.*

Motherwort, as one would expect from the name, is an effective treatment for many female disorders and is particularly valuable as an emmenagogue (induces or increases menstrual flow). It is also a good heart and general tonic and is recommended for calming sufferers from hysteria.

Use the whole herb, cut in August and dried. It may be taken as a decoction or strong infusion, 25 g/1 oz of herb to 600 ml/1 pt/2½ cups of water. The dose is 150 ml/¼ pt/⅔ cup 4 times a day, so the whole 600 ml/1 pt/2½ cups is drunk in a day. However, motherwort makes a very bitter drink and in the old days it was often given as a more palatable syrup.

MUGWORT *Artemisia vulgaris*

> ***Warning!***
> *Not to be used by pregnant women.*

Mugwort is known as the 'traveller's herb', and in times past was believed to afford protection during a journey against weariness, sunstroke, wild beasts and unfriendly spirits. Before the introduction of hops, it was employed to flavour beer and other drinks. The herb is recommended as an appetiser and an aid to digestion, and as a sedative. The parts of the herb used are the roots and leaves. Its principal application today – combined with pennyroyal and southernwood – is as an emmenagogue (to induce or increase mentrual flow).

MYRRH *Commiphora myrrha*

> ***Warning!***
> *Not to be used by pregnant women.*

Myrrh oil mixed with bicarbonate of soda makes a good toothpaste.

Rub myrrh oil on to gums if suffering from gingivitis.

Myrrh is an emmenagogue (induces menstruation).
All from Cylch Cyhiraeth

NETTLE, GREATER *Urtica dioica*

Stinging nettles – for which no great search is required! – have been used over the years in a hundred ways. The Romans rubbed them on to their limbs to improve the circulation in cold weather. The Scots wove cloth from the fibre of old nettle stalks. Country people made nettle beer which, in addition to being a pleasant beverage, was drunk by the elderly to ease the pain of gout and rheumatism.

The plant can also be eaten as a vegetable in the spring: gather (wearing gloves!) the young tops when they are 15–20 cm/6–8 in tall. Wash in running water and place in a saucepan, dripping, without any extra water. Cook, with the lid on, for about 20 minutes. Add a little salt, pepper and butter.

An infusion of nettles has long been valued as a purifier of the blood. Nettle tea made from the roots was believed to have diuretic properties, particularly beneficial to those suffering from water retention or kidney problems.

The plant is much disliked by flies. To keep these pests out of the kitchen, hang up a bunch of nettles in the area.

 When people have been stung by nettles they often rush around looking for dock leaves to rub on the affected part. The best antidote for nettle stings, however, is nettle sap. Cut a nettle stem through and a small amount of sap will appear. Squeeze the stem (through a tissue or muslin) to get more sap.

Chris Bray

The juice of fresh nettles arrests nosebleeds, as does lemon juice. Place the liquid on cotton wool and hold against the nostrils.

Sylvia Guyatt

Nettle syrup (made from a very old recipe) is said to be a most effective blood purifier. It also provides a cooling drink when diluted with soda water.

To make: gather the tops of young nettles and wash well. Place in a large pan and add 1.2 litres/2 pts/5 cups of water for every 450 g/ 1 lb of nettles. Boil for 1 hour then strain and add 450 g/1 lb/2 cups of sugar to every 600 ml/ 1 pt/2½ cups of juice. Boil the mixture for 30 minutes, then cool and put into sterile screw-top jars.

Linda Bruce

When watering plants, add some nettles to the water in the can. The herb is a good fertiliser.

It is not generally a good idea to pick nettles after midsummer, by which time they have

grown tough and bitter. But if a laxative is what
you seek, then nettles gathered after 21 June
and cooked and eaten as a vegetable will prove
most effective!

Cylch Cyhiraeth

NIGHTSHADE, BLACK *Solanum nigrum*

> **Warning!**
> *This plant is dangerous: use only with expert guidance.*

The poisonous black nightshade, common in the south of
England and found less frequently elsewhere, springs up on
verges and waste ground, particularly in damp shady
places. The plant is also known as the garden nightshade as
it often grows in cultivated areas. Its leaves possess powerful narcotic properties, and in Bohemia are hung in cradles
to make their occupants sleepy.

An infusion of black nightshade (using 1–2 grains of
dried leaves (1 grain = 0.065 g) was in the past recommended to cause a fever to 'break', thus allowing the suf-
ferer to sweat away the infection. In very small doses, the
herb is said to be beneficial in cases of skin diseases. Fresh
leaves are sometimes applied externally to relieve pain.

It is also a magic plant, an infusion of whose leaves is
said to assist in revealing a person's true wishes for the
future: sprinkle the liquid on to the body and around the
room.

OAK, COMMON *Quercus robur*

An infusion of oak blossom will ease the pain of
arthritis. It will also help aching feet.

Cylch Cyhiraeth

OLIVE *Olea europaea*

Olive oil is good for rheumatic joints. Drink
5 ml/1 tsp of olive oil daily and rub the oil on to
the affected parts when sitting down to rest.

Sylvia Guyatt

ONION *Allium cepa*

For coughs and mild bronchitis, slice a large onion finely and cover it with 45–60 ml/3–4 tbsp of demerara sugar. Leave to stand for a few hours and then drink the juice that has been produced.

If symptoms persist, consult your doctor.

Linda Bruce

'If any be sick of infection, skin 1 or 2 onions and place by their bed. Keep changing these. Do not eat these onions. Burn them, but if an evil wisher asks for them, give them freely, or better, let them take the onions without asking.'

old *Book of Shadows* via *Patricia Crowther*

For nettle and bee stings, apply raw cut onion. Elder leaves are also good for this.

Sylvia Guyatt

PARSLEY *Carum petroselinum*

> **Warning!**
> *Parsley can cause miscarriages if eaten in large amounts, so pregnant women should not use it.*

Parsley leaves are, of course, a familiar sight on the dinner table, being much used by cooks as an appetiser and as garnish for savoury dishes. The herb also possesses the unusual ability to dispel strong scents, and is credited with the power to render even garlic almost odourless when the two are mixed together.

Medicinally, it is a valuable diuretic (in the form of a strong decoction of the root) especially where water retention is associated with kidney disorders. In the Great War, parsley tea was found to be most beneficial to soldiers in the trenches with kidney complaints resulting from dysentery. Oil extracted from the seeds – which is also present in the roots to a lesser degree – is a good, safe emmenagogue (induces or increases mentrual flow). Parsley is also recommended as an expectorant (promotes the expulsion of mucus from the respiratory passages).

Parsley is a good emergency dressing for wounds. Crush the herb and lay on the wound. Cover lightly.

Sylvia Guyatt

PENNYROYAL *Mentha pulegium*

> **Warning!**
> *This herb should not be taken during pregnancy.*

Pennyroyal, a variety of mint, has a sedative effect. It also induces perspiration at the onset of a cold, promotes menstruation and is useful for treating nausea and nervous complaints. Native Americans (Indians) use pennyroyal to treat headaches.

Preparation and dosage: make an infusion of 5 ml/1 tsp of the herb with 250 ml/8 fl oz/1 cup of hot water. Take 1–2 cups a day.

Kim Tracey

Pennyroyal has been renowned for centuries for its flea-repelling powers. In Roman times, Pliny named it *pulegium*, *pulex* being the Latin word for flea. Gather little bunches of the plant (stem and leaves) just before the plant flowers. These are strewn about the house. The herb contains oil of pulegium, which fleas dislike.

Less well known is the fact that pennyroyal possesses powerful anti-ant properties! Cut a stem of the herb in half and draw a line on the ground with the sap: the ants will not cross it.

Jackie James

POKE ROOT *Phytolacca decandra*

> **Warning!**
> *This has narcotic properties and should only be used under the care of a qualified herbalist. It should only be used in conjunction with orthodox medical treatment, not as an alternative.*

Poke root (a perennial found in North America and Mediterranean countries, though hardy enough to grow happily in the UK), is one of the most powerful herbs to use externally against ulcerations.

The root should be unearthed in autumn or spring, cleaned and split lengthways, and dried. The fresh leaves and berries may be used instead. Make into an aqueous solution and apply externally thrice daily.

PUMPKIN *Cucurbita pepo*

Pumpkin seed paste will help to heal wounds, particularly in cases of minor burns and chapped skin. Grind up the seeds in a coffee grinder to produce a paste.

Kim Tracey

RASPBERRY *Rubus idaeus*

Raspberry leaf tea, a stimulant, is frequently recommended in herbals as a aid during pregnancy and childbirth. It can be drunk freely during pregnancy and birth, and is said to ease childbirth. Make the tea with 25 g/1 oz of fresh raspberry leaves to 600 ml/1 pt/2½ cups boiling water.

Cylch Cyhiraeth

ROSEMARY *Rosmarinus officinalis*

Rosemary tea, made from the young shoots (including the flowers), increases mental alertness, so is useful in preparing for events such as job interviews or examinations.

In times past rosemary had a reputation for improving memory, which accounts for its adoption as the symbol of true love and the saying 'Rosemary for remembrance'. Another old belief is that where rosemary flourishes, the woman rules.

Rosemary tea is also a good remedy for headaches and nervous depression, and taken warm, eases colic. The herb is also recommended as an antispasmodic (prevents or arrests spasms) and antiseptic.

An infusion of the dried plant mixed with borax and used cold makes an excellent hairwash, which is also effective against dandruff.

ROWAN *Sorbus aucuparia*

Fresh juice from the rowan fruit will soothe inflamed mucous membrane and so is good for hoarseness and sore throats; make a solution and gargle. The juice will also act as a mild laxative. The fruit, made into a jam, becomes astringent and can be eaten to treat mild diarrhoea.

Dosage: take 5 ml/1 tsp of fresh juice as and when needed.

Kim Tracey

RUE *Ruta graveolens*

> **Warning!**
> *Rue is poisonous if taken to excess, so great caution in its use is called for.*

Rue is one of the oldest garden plants, having been brought to Britain by the Romans who believed it to be beneficial to the eyesight. Its leaves have a strong, unpleasant odour and a bitter nauseous taste. The parts of the plant used – either fresh or dry – are the tops of the young shoots, picked before flowering. They are usually made into infusions or decoctions.

The herb is recommended as a remedy for palpitations associated with the menopause; a leaf or two may be chewed for this purpose. It also acts on the womb, being an emmenagogue (inducing or increasing menstrual flow) when a warm infusion of the herb is drunk, and inducing uterine contractions.

SAGE *Salvia officinalis*

> **Warning!**
> *Not to be used by pregnant women.*

An infusion of sage leaves, for use either as a mouthwash or a gargle, is an excellent antiseptic for mouth and throat infections such as tonsillitis, bleeding gums, mouth ulcers and an inflamed sore throat. A strong infusion of the herb makes a beneficial lotion for cleansing open ulcers and skin abrasions. Sage tea (made by pouring 600 ml/1 pt/2½ cups of boiling water on to 25 g/1 oz of the dried herb) has a stimulatory effect on the stomach and intestines. Place 1–3 drops of sage oil on a tissue and sniff occasionally to help clear congested respiratory tubes. But be warned: if inhaled continually it is said to cause lightheadedness and dizziness. Sage is an emmenagogue (induces menstruation). There is an old saying that, unlike rosemary, sage flourishes where the man is king of the castle.

> To clean teeth, rub sage leaves on them.
>
> *Cylch Cyhiraeth*

> Sage leaves can be used to cleanse and strengthen the gums. Massage with a few washed leaves.
>
> *Patricia Crowther*

> Sage stain-removing toothpowder may be made by placing 30 ml/2 tbsp of fresh sage leaves and 30 ml/2 tbsp of sea salt in a bowl and crushing them to a fine powder. Place the mixture on a tray and cook in a warm oven. When it is well baked (fairly hard), remove from the oven and pulverise again. Store in a shallow airtight tin.

> For colds and throaty coughs, make a strong tea using sage leaves.
>
> *Both from Linda Bruce*

SCULLCAP, COMMON *Scutellaria galericulata* (English)
SCULLCAP, VIRGINIAN *Scutellaria lateriflora* (American)

Warning!
An overdose of this herb can cause symptoms similar to an epileptic fit.

This herb is famous for being an excellent nervine (having a soothing or calming effect on the nerves). The American variety is known popularly as 'mad-dog scullcap', since it was used in cases of rabies. The whole herb is used, gathered in June, dried and powdered. The usual dose is an infusion of 25 g/1 oz of powdered herb to 600 ml/1 pt/ 2½ cups of boiling water, a ½ teacupful to be taken every few hours.

Scullcap brings relief to those suffering from convulsions, St Vitus's Dance, hysteria and severe attacks of hiccoughs. It also relaxes the restless and may be taken as an emmenagogue (to induce or increase menstrual flow).

SHEPHERD'S PURSE *Capsella bursa-pastoris*

The juice of shepherd's purse, also known as pickpocket, when dropped in the ears will relieve pain, noises and wax.

If ear pain persists, consult your doctor.

Sylvia Guyatt

SOAPWORT *Saponaria officinalis*

As a lotion, fresh soapwort is good for treating inflammatory skin disease such as simple herpes.

Sylvia Guyatt

Soapwort will help with skin conditions such as eczema. Wash with a mild infusion of the herb. Soapwort should be used fresh, not dried.

Cylch Cyhiraeth

To make soapwort washing lather: place a bunch of soapwort leaves in a pan and cover with cold rainwater. Bring to the boil and simmer for 3–4 minutes. Remove from the heat, cover and cool. When cold, press through a strainer and pour into a sterile screw-top bottle.

To use: mix sufficient soapwort washing liquid with warmed rainwater to form a lather. Wash silks, lace and other delicate fabrics in the liquid. As well as getting them clean, the

soapwort imparts a lovely sheen and softness to
the materials.

Linda Bruce

STRAWBERRY

Rub teeth with a strawberry to remove plaque,
clean teeth and whiten them.

Linda Bruce

SUNFLOWER *Helianthus annuus*

The sunflower is an amazingly generous plant, nearly every
part of it providing a substance useful to someone! Its
fibrous stems may be made into paper; its leaves are a nutri-
tious cattle food; its flowers contain a yellow dye; and its
seeds, when pressed, yield a sweet-tasting oil similar to olive
oil.

Uncrushed, the seeds are also eaten by many, both animal and human. In America, women wishing to conceive
chew sunflower seeds. In Russian the seeds are sold in the
street, rather as roasted chestnuts are in Britain. In Portugal
they are ground to make bread.

Birds of all kinds are fond of the seeds which, if bruised
and given to chicken, increase their laying power. Bees love
sunflowers, which are rich in nectar.

A remedy to relieve whooping cough can be made by
browning sunflower seeds in the oven and then making an
infusion with them.

Always consult your doctor in cases of any severe cough.

THYME, GARDEN *Thymus vulgaris*

The herb contains the potent antiseptic thymol which can
either be taken internally (with caution) or applied to the
skin. An infusion made from thyme leaves may be used as a
mouthwash or, in the case of sore throats, as a gargle. It
makes a good antiseptic lotion for burns, broken chilblains
and skin diseases such as eczema and psoriasis.

Internally it is effective against intestinal parasites, but
should only be given to strong adults, as large doses are
required. So far as disorders of the stomach are concerned,

thyme is recommended for gastritis and loss of appetite. On the pulmonary side, it is employed as an expectorant (to promote the expulsion of mucus from the respiratory passages). It also has valuable properties as a general tonic.

When faced with a troublesome situation, taking a bath in water to which you have added a few sprigs of thyme will magically build up courage.

Bees are particularly fond of thyme, and it is said that if hives are located in an area where the plant grows in plenty, then the honey they produce will possess a rare sweetness and flavour. Alternatively, plant thyme near the hives!

Add a few drops of thyme essential oil to a canful of water to rid your plants of greenfly.

Cylch Cyhiraeth

Thyme disinfectant is particularly useful for wiping down kitchen and bathroom surfaces. Use it neat. Make by pouring 600 ml/1 pt/ 2½ cups of boiling water over 25 g/1 oz of fresh thyme leaves and leaving the brew to steep for 10 minutes. Strain and cool; pour into sterile screw-top jars and seal.

Linda Bruce

VALERIAN *Valeriana officinalis*

Valerian has been called by many names over the centuries, but perhaps the most expressive is the Greek *phu*, which is how the ancient herbalists described their reaction to the plant's offensive smell! However, one of its synonyms was 'heal-all', so maybe fragrance isn't everything.

The part used is the root. Make a decoction with it; see Chapter 2, page 27 for instructions on how to make a decoction and the dosage. This has a powerful sedative effect on those who are afflicted with diseases of the nervous system such as St Vitus's Dance and neuralgia. It also calms, thus being beneficial in cases of hypochondria, nervous overstrain and other similar disorders. It encourages sleep in insomniacs. Exercise caution, however, since taking too much can cause headache, a 'heavy head' or stupor.

VERVAIN *Verbena officinalis*

This herb, which is best gathered at midsummer, has a strong occult tradition behind it. Vervain in its magical capacity is used as a purification and protection incense, and for love and fertility charms. Medicinally, it was valued as a remedy for kidney stones and other renal diseases. It is still used as a diuretic and is a good tonic to combat nervous wear and tear.

It is also recommended for some problems of the digestive tract; for example, where a purgative has been taken, vervain will ease the resulting intestinal pain. Applied externally, the herb will bring relief to those with piles.

Preparation and dosage: take as a tea. Pour 250 ml/ 8 fl oz/1 cup boiling water over about 10 ml/2 tsp of dried vervain (the whole plant) and let it infuse for 10 minutes. Drink twice a day. The brew is bitter in taste and may be sweetened with honey.

WITCH HAZEL *Hamamelis virginiana*

This shrub grows in Canada and the eastern United States. The parts used are the leaves, fresh or dried. Since it grows in North America, making your own preparation is not really practicable in Britain. However, witch hazel (an extract of the leaves diluted with water) is obtainable from any chemist. Witch hazel is particularly beneficial to the reproductive system: a decoction will help sufferers from menorrhagia (excessive mentrual bleeding), and those run-down after a termination or miscarriage.

Applied externally, it makes a most refreshing facial lotion and if dabbed on insect bites will speedily soothe and reduce the swelling.

It is said that a few leaves added to the bath water bestows allure!

> To make an eyewash, use equal parts of witch
> hazel and water. Bathe eyes.
>
> *Sylvia Guyatt*

WORMWOOD *Artemisia absinthium*

This plant, together with rue, are the bitterest herbs there are. Nevertheless, wormwood has long been valued as a stomachic (stimulates gastric activity); a light infusion of leaves and flowery tops (fresh) is particularly efficacious as an appetiser, aids digestion and relieves flatulence. Beware of making the infusion too strong, however, as this causes nausea.

Wormwood is also known as a nervine tonic (having a soothing or calming effect on the nerves), being helpful in cases of depression. It will also increase vitality. The liqueur absinthe, which is based on an extract from wormwood, is said to be valuable as a 'mental restorative', in particular having a calming effect on those of a nervous disposition. Make an infusion (not too strong) and take small amounts (a wineglassful) through the day, warm then cold, with breakfast, lunch and supper, and for elevenses, at teatime and late evening.

The herb is also recommended as a remedy for a poorly-functioning gall bladder. In the case of jaundice, it helps to reduce yellowness of the skin.

In both the latter cases, consult your doctor if symptoms persist.

YARROW *Achillea millefolium*

From ancient times this herb has been used in love and marriage charms. Taken to a wedding ceremony, it is traditionally believed that it will bestow upon a couple seven years of happiness.

As a mouthwash, yarrow is of benefit for toothache.

Yarrow ointment is excellent for stopping the flow of blood, as well as being a very good antiseptic.

To make: take 50 g/2 oz of dried yarrow leaves, 75 g/3 oz/¹/₃ cup of coconut fat or oil and 15 g/¹/₂ oz of beeswax. Simmer these together for 1¹/₂ hours over a low heat. The more slowly it is prepared, the better and stronger the ointment will be.

Both from Sylvia Guyatt

A yarrow hair tonic may be made by pouring 1.2 litres/2 pts/5 cups of boiling water over 2 handfuls of dried yarrow leaves and flowers and simmering the mixture for 10–15 minutes. Add 1.2 litres/2 pts/5 cups of white wine vinegar and infuse for 24 hours. Strain and pour into sterile screw-top jars. This hair tonic is good for mild dandruff and to discourage premature baldness.

Linda Bruce

❧4❧

MULTIPLE-HERB
REMEDIES

This chapter concentrates on remedies which are made with more than one herb, often several herbs.

The remedies have different uses – medicinal, cosmetic, culinary, as household preparations and for magic – so they are divided into these sections for ease of reference and use.

Remember, if you need any guidance on the general principles of making teas, infusions, syrups, ointments, poultices or compresses, refer back to Chapter 2, pages 27–28.

Safety warnings on the use of certain herbs or remedies appear at the beginning of the individual recipes.

MEDICINAL REMEDIES

A COUGH MEDICINE

This cough medicine tastes horrible but is most effective!

600 ml/1 pt/2¹/₂ cups water (from a spring if possible)
30 ml/2 tbsp malt extract
15 ml/1 tbsp wild flower honey
4 tops white horehound *Marrubium vulgare* (i.e. the top section of the plant, about the top 7.5 cm/ 3 in, which comprises the soft, newly grown stem and newly opened leaves)
2–3 pinches dried coltsfoot *Tussilago farfara*
1 pinch dried thyme *Thymus vulgaris*

A few fresh chamomile flowers *Anthemis nobilis*
2 drops pine essential oil *or*
2 drops eucalyptus essential oil

Add the honey and the malt extract to the water and bring to the boil. Reduce the heat so that the liquid simmers. Add the white horehound, coltsfoot, thyme and chamomile flowers and continue to simmer with the lid off the pan, so that the liquid reduces in volume. Strain, let it cool, then add the essential oil. The dose is 15 ml/1 tbsp of the medicine, which may be taken as often as required.

Cylch Cyhiraeth

HONEY COUGH MIXTURE

100 g/4 oz/¹⁄₂ cup pure cod liver oil
25 g/1 oz/2 tbsp glycerine
100 g/4 oz/¹⁄₂ cup honey
Strained juice of 3 lemons

Put all the ingredients into a sterile screw-top jar and shake well. Take the mixture 3 times a day after meals. Always shake the jar well before use.

Linda Bruce

OLD COUNTRY COUGH CURE

Stick of liquorice
50 g/2 oz fine linseed (flax seed)
50 g/2 oz/¹/₄ cup sugar candy
24 raisins
900 ml/1¹/₂ pts/3³/₄ cups water
Juice of 1 large lemon

Place all the ingredients in a saucepan and simmer, with the lid on, then strain and add the lemon juice. Cool, then pour into screw-top jars. Take 2–3 teaspoonfuls every 4 hours.

Linda Bruce

For a cold: RASPBERRY VINEGAR

1.1 kg/2¹/₂ lb raspberries
2.25 litres/4 pts/10 cups white wine vinegar
450 g/1 lb/2 cups sugar to each 1.2 litres/2 pts/5
   cups liquid

Pick 1.1 kg/2¹/₂ lb of raspberries and pour over them 2.25 litres/4 pts/10 cups of white wine vinegar. Leave to stand for 3–4 days, then strain and add 450 g/1 lb/2 cups of sugar for every 1.2 litres/2 pts/5 cups of liquid. Simmer the mixture until the sugar dissolves (do not allow it to boil), cool, then pour into sterile screw-top jars. Take 10 ml/2 tsp for a cold.

Blackberry vinegar may be made in the same way and is also good for a cold.

Linda Bruce

For sore throats: ROSE SYRUP

Rose syrup is an excellent cure for sore throats and is also a very good pick-me-up.

> **450 g/1 lb rhubarb**
> **600 ml/1 pt/2½ cups cold water**
> **350 g/12 oz/1½ cups white sugar**
> **Petals of 7 red roses**

Cut up the rhubarb, cover with the cold water, bring to the boil and simmer until all the juice is extracted. Strain. Add the white sugar and rose petals to the liquid. Simmer the mixture gently for 15 minutes, strain out the petals and boil until the syrup thickens. It will be a rich red colour. Pour into warmed screw-top jars and seal.

To make a good drink, put 5 ml/1 tsp of the syrup into a mug and dissolve it in 15 ml/1 tbsp of boiling water. When it has cooled, fill up with milk.

Linda Bruce

For sores and bruises: FARMHOUSE HERB SALVE

This excellent salve is for all sores and bruises.

> **450 g/1 lb/2 cups lard**
> **1 good handful elderflowers, wormwood and**
> **groundsel (preferably fresh)**

Take the lard and place it in an earthenware pot with the elderflowers, wormwood and groundsel. Bring to the boil in the oven and simmer for half an hour. Then strain and pour into screw-top jars. Dried herbs may be used for the salve, but fresh are best.

Linda Bruce

FOR SKIN IRRITATIONS
(e.g. chickenpox, prickly heat)

Equal quantities chickweed, mint and marigold leaves

❧

Wash well and make an infusion. When cooled, keep in the fridge and gently apply to the affected parts with cotton wool.

Linda Bruce

FOR HOT FLUSHES

5 ml/1 tsp dried sage
5 ml/1 tsp dried motherwort

❧

Make an infusion from the herbs and take as a drink when needed. Particularly useful for women going through the menopause.

Linda Bruce

FOR PALPITATIONS

Equal parts fresh or dried valerian, lemon balm, hawthorn and motherwort

❧

Make an infusion from the herbs and take as a drink when needed.

Linda Bruce

FOR PERIOD PAINS

10 ml/2 tsp dried tansy *Tanacetum vulgare*
10 ml/2 tsp dried pennyroyal *Mentha pulegium*
10 ml/2 tsp dried rue *Ruta graveolens*

Make an infusion with 600 ml/1 pt/2½ cups water and the dried herbs and take as a drink when needed. This will relieve period pains.

Cylch Cyhiraeth

STOMACH SETTLER

10 ml/2 tsp dill seed *Pecedanum graveolens*
5 ml/1 tsp dried fennel *Foeniculum vulgare*
5 ml/1 tsp dried peppermint or spearmint *Mentha piperita* or *Mentha viridis*

Make an infusion and take as a drink when needed. This brew helps relieve nausea, uncomfortable stomach cramps and stomach upsets. It can also be taken by nursing mothers to help increase the production of breast milk.

Chris Sempers

A HEADACHE TEA

15 ml/1 tbsp white willow bark *Salix alba*
2.5 ml/½ tsp valerian root (chipped) *Valeriana officinalis*
10 ml/2 tsp dried passion flower *Passiflora incarnata*
10 ml/2 tsp dried common or Virginia scullcap
Scutellaria galericulata or *Scutellaria lateriflora*

Put all the ingredients into a teapot, fill the pot with boiling water, let it stand for 20 minutes, then drink.

Cylch Cyhiraeth

TRANQUILLITY TEA

This brew is not a tranquilliser, but it is very useful in times of great stress, or when clear thinking is needed (such as when closing a business deal).

> **30 ml/2 tbsp dried lemon balm** *Melissa officinalis*
> **5 ml/1 tsp dried chamomile** *Anthemis nobilis*
> **20 ml/4 tsp dried lemon grass** *Cymbopogon citratus*
> **5 ml/1 tsp dried spearmint** *Mentha viridis*
> **5 ml/1 tsp grated orange peel**

❧

Use 5 ml/1 tsp of the combined mixture in a cup or mug and brew for 5 minutes.

Chris Sempers

ADDICTION BREAKER

> **Warning!**
> *This brew should be avoided by pregnant women, as it can
> also help to bring on a period and regularise menstruation.*

*This brew helps to relieve the worst symptoms of withdrawal,
whether from drugs, alcohol or an oppressive mental situation. It
tastes particularly nasty, but in this case that seems to help!*

15 ml/1 tbsp dried common or Virginian scullcap
Scutellaria galericulata or *Scutellaria lateriflora*
10 ml/2 tsp dried sage *Salvia officinalis*
5 ml/1 tsp dried yarrow *Achillea millefolium*
5 ml/1 tsp dried parsley *Carum petroselium*

❧

Pour 600 ml/1 pt/2½ cups boiling water over the
ingredients and leave to brew for 5–10 minutes. Strain
and take a cupful as required through the day, up to
600 ml/1 pt/2½ cups a day. After a fortnight stop for two
weeks, then start again if necessary.

Chris Sempers

CULINARY REMEDY

WINTER CORDIAL

30 ml/2 tbsp fine oatmeal
1 lemon
2.5 ml/½ tsp ground ginger
15 ml/1 tbsp demerara sugar
1.2 litres/2 pts/5 cups boiling water

❧

Mix together the oatmeal, sugar and ground ginger.
Grate the rind of the lemon and add. Gradually pour
on the boiling water while stirring. Put in a saucepan, add
the juice of the lemon and simmer for 10 minutes. Strain and
serve hot.

Linda Bruce

COSMETIC REMEDIES

A GOOD SKIN CLEANSER

These ingredients combine well to produce a good skin cleanser and tonic.

1 part burdock leaves *Arctium lappa*
1 part sweet cicely *Myrrhis odorata*
A few drops of myrrh oil

Boil the burdock leaves and sweet cicely together and add the myrrh oil when the liquid has cooled.

Cylch Cyhiraeth

ELDERFLOWER FACEWASH CLEANSER

Handful each of:
elderflowers *Sambucus nigra*
lavender *Lavandula vera*
toadflax *Linaria vulgaris*
rose petals
Handful each of marigold and chamomile flowers
     (optional)
600 ml/1 pt/2½ cups of water
15 ml/1 tbsp wild flower honey
5 ml/1 tsp vegetable glycerine

Boil the water (on its own) for 5 minutes, remove the pan from the heat, add all the ingredients and simmer for 15–20 minutes. Strain and use.

Because it is water-based, this lotion does not last for very long. Alternatively the recipe may be made up as an ointment.

Cylch Cyhiraeth

SOFTENING SKIN LOTION

If you have grated and squeezed lemons for other purposes, use the husks to make a softening skin lotion.

> **Husks of 1–2 grated and squeezed lemons, roughly cut up**
> **25 g/1 oz/¹/₄ cup powdered borax**
> **50 g/2 oz/¹/₄ cup glycerine**
> **120 ml/4 fl oz/¹/₂ cup boiling water**

Steep the lemon husks in the boiling water and, when it has cooled, pour it off. Dissolve the borax in the lemon water and add the glycerine. Pour into sterile screw-top jars.

Linda Bruce

ROMANY HAIR TONIC

> **1 juicy onion**
> **120 ml/4 fl oz/¹/₂ cup rum**

Dice the onion and steep in the rum for 36 hours. Strain and pour into sterile screw-top jars.

Linda Bruce

TO MAKE HAIR GROW

1 eggcupful rum
25 g/1 oz/2 tbsp beef marrow
10 ml/2 tsp castor oil
15 ml/1 tbsp/¹/₂ oz dried rosemary
20 drops paraffin
2.5 ml/¹/₂ tsp white wax

Mix all the ingredients together and rub into the scalp well with a flannel for 15 minutes. Leave for 8 hours and then gently wash off. Apply every other day.

Rubbing the scalp with onion juice several times a week is said to be another way of restoring hair. You may need to experiment with the amounts of the ingredients.

Linda Bruce

REDUCING BATH MIX

> **Warning!**
> *Do not massage on or near your breasts with this mix.*

100 g/4 oz/1 cup bicarbonate of soda
100 g/4 oz/1 cup borax
30 ml/2 tbsp glycerine
100 g/4 oz/1 cup kitchen salt
8 tbsp powdered alum* *Geranium maculatum*
　*Parts used: leaves, dried rhizome. For
　maximum benefit: dig up the roots before the
　plant flowers or collect the leaves before the
　plant seeds.

Place all the ingredients in a pan, pour on 1.75 litres/3 pts boiling water and stir until they have all dissolved.

Then add the liquid to your (warm) bath water. Wallow in the bath for 20 minutes, then stand up and towel yourself briskly until the skin feels nicely toned. Get into the bath again, lie back and, while your body is submerged, grip your flesh between your thumb and middle finger and lift in a plucking motion. Lift and release your flesh in this way all over until you have treated all the fatty parts of your body, avoiding the breasts and breast area. Finally, soap your body and massage with a loofah, using brisk circular movements.

All this could make you feel tired, so it is best to take the treatment just before bed. It is said that many pounds may be shed in this way: the bath may be taken every other night.

Linda Bruce

HOUSEHOLD REMEDIES

TO KEEP MOTHS AWAY

100 g/4 oz/1 cup clove pink leaves
Grated peel of 3 oranges
25 g/1 oz/¹/₄ cup fresh thyme leaves

❧

Clove pink leaves are from the carnation family and have a perfume similar to cloves. Mix them with the grated peel of the oranges and the thyme leaves. Dry in an airy place.

Place muslin sachets of the mixture in drawers and wardrobes to keep away moths and scent garments.

Pauline Newbery

MAGIC REMEDIES

CLAIRVOYANCE ENHANCER BREW

This brew can be used at any time prior to scrying, divination, magical dreaming or when trying to make contact with other worldly entities.

> **30 ml/2 tbsp dried hops** *Humulus lupulus*
> **5 ml/1 tsp dried uva ursi** *Arctostaphylos uva-ursi*
> **10 ml/2 tsp dried anise** *Pimpinella anisum*
> **10 ml/2 tsp dried bugleweed** *Lycopus virginicus*
> **10 ml/2 tsp dried hyssop** *Hyssopus officinalis*
> **10 ml/2 tsp dried kava kava** *Piper methysticum*
> **10 ml/2 tsp dried marigold** *Calendula officinalis*
> **5 ml/1 tsp linseed (flax seed)** *Linum usitatissimum*

Mix the ingredients well and grind the whole mixture finely. Use 5 ml/1 tsp of the mixture in a cup or mug of boiling water. Leave to brew for at least 5 minutes. The drink may be sweetened with honey.

The only side effects (if the whole of the above mixture were drunk sitting at one sitting) would be a tendency to fall asleep; the brew might also act as a laxative.

Chris Sempers

LOVE POTION

> **15 ml/1 tbsp red rose petals (highly scented)**
> **5 ml/1 tsp powdered liquorice root** *Glycyrrhiza glabra*
> **1 pinch powdered coriander seed** *Coriandrum sativum*
> **5 ml/1 tsp dried lemon balm** *Melissa officinalis*

Powder the mixture well. It can then either be taken as a tea by two lovers (a loving cup) or a pinch can be added to the food of the one you desire for a lover. Take care: if you both partake, you will both be smitten; if only one partakes, your love may not be reciprocated.

Chris Sempers

❧5❧

ESSENTIAL OILS

Essential oils, the essences of flowers, leaves, barks, roots and berries, have been valued for their therapeutic powers for many centuries. Their extraction is not, however, something that can easily be undertaken at home.

The simplest method, called *enfleurage*, involves soaking 3–4 batches of strongly scented flowers or leaves in a vegetable oil over a period of several days, and produces a scented rather than a true essential oil. Nor does it necessarily follow that the scented petals treated in this way will produce oil that smells of that flower; the result is sometimes quite different.

The least complicated way of extracting the true essence of a plant also takes a long time and produces only a tiny amount of oil. To obtain this, take some highly perfumed flowers, place them in a shallow dish and cover them with rainwater. Stand the dish in a sunny place for several days and a film should gradually appear on the surface of the water. This is the essential oil of the flower.

The usual commercial method of extracting essential oils is by steam distillation and it is not really possible for the average person to do this at home.

All in all, the most convenient way to acquire essential oils is to buy them from a health food shop, herbalist or occult supplier. The names and addresses of a number of such companies which provide a mail order service appear in the Source List on page 113. Take care to ensure that what you buy is a pure, high-quality essential oil; if it is diluted in a solvent or mixed with an artificial substance it will not have the desired effect.

Synthetic oils, which are used in commercial cosmetics and perfumes, have no beneficial properties, and if they are included in incense, they will smell revoltingly of their coal-tar origins when burned.

HOW TO USE ESSENTIAL OILS

Oils at bathtime

• One of the most pleasant ways of using essential oils is in the bath. Add 5–10 drops of oil to the water when it has been run.

• To heighten psychic powers, add a selection of the following oils when you bathe: acacia, cinnamon, clove, honeysuckle, lemon grass, nutmeg, patchouli, peppermint, rose, thyme, yarrow. Orange peel may also be added.

• For an aphrodisiac bath, include some of these oils: acacia, apple, chamomile, catnip, geranium, hibiscus, jasmine, lavender, lemon balm, lovage, myrtle, orchid, rosemary, rose, thyme, vervain. (Have your bath before going to meet a lover, or share it with your partner!)

• Basil, carnation, lavender and rosemary will boost energy when added to the bath water.

• A healing bath would include a selection of the following: allspice, carnation, cedar, cinnamon, heliotrope, lavender, lemon balm, lime, peppermint, rose, rosemary, sandalwood, thyme and violet.

Make your own bath salts

Bath salts are very easy to prepare and the homemade variety is much to be preferred to any available in the shops, which are full of chemicals.

Mix together equal parts of table salt, bicarbonate of soda and Epsom salts. Add your choice of essential oils drop by drop and stir until the whole compound is thoroughly moistened. Colour may be added, if you wish, using food dyes. (Blend colours before you add them to the salts, otherwise the effect will be two-tone!)

Add magic – with colour

Colour magic is really a separate subject, but a few

examples are given here:
- Light blue for healing, tranquillity
- Dark blue for flexibility, the submerged mind
- Green for fertility, prosperity, good luck
- White for purification, peace
- Red for health, passion, courage.

Sprinkle about 30 ml/2 tbsp of the salts into a bath.

THE MEDICINAL USE OF OILS

So far as the medicinal properties of essential oils are concerned, Kim Tracey has contributed the following list of herbs, which may also be burned as incense.

One way of absorbing the oil is to place a few drops in a vapouriser so that it becomes part of a room's atmosphere. Another is by inhalation, which is used most often for headaches, tension and blocked sinuses. Place 10 drops of essential oil in a basin containing about 100 ml/3½ fl oz/ 6½ tbsp of hot water, put a towel over your head, lean over the basin and breathe in deeply until the scent fades. Repeat 3 times a day.

An even simpler method is to put 10 drops of oil on a handkerchief and breath from it frequently. If a handkerchief sprinkled with camphor or menthol is placed on your pillow at night, it will keep your nose clear while you sleep.

OILS AND THEIR PROPERTIES

- For general good health: cinnamon, myrrh, cloves, nutmeg, balm, frankincense
- For nervous ailments: absinthe, fennel, aloe
- For the digestive system: mallow, vervain, clover
- For cardiac problems: geranium, sage
- For circulatory disorders: orchid
- For hepatic ailments: lily, narcissus
- For the lymphatic system: lotus, comfrey
- For procreation: comfrey, birthwort
- For renal problems: gladiolus, absinthe
- Cerebral: pimpernel, sunflower, cyclamen
- For colds etc. (to clear the head, for nasal congestion): camphor, menthol

TRY AROMATHERAPY

Warning!
Pregnant women should avoid the herbs basil, rosemary, thyme, juniper, sage, hyssop, cinnamon and myrrh. Aromatherapists and herbalists also advise that it is best not to take essential oils internally except under the care of a qualified practitioner.

Aromatherapy is another way of gaining the therapeutic benefits of essential oils. It is usually thought of as body massage with essential oils, though the term may also include other methods of absorption, such as those outlined above.

When used as a body massage the plant essence is diluted in a carrier oil such as sweet almond oil.

Raven, run by Chris Sempers and her husband Graham Raven (see Source List on page 113) carry a good selection of essential and ready-blended aromatherapy oils intended to help with a whole range of problems such as anxiety, arthritis, asthma, hayfever, hot flushes, PMT and rheumatism.

❧6❧

GOOD SENSE AND INCENSE:

BY KEITH MORGAN

Warning!
It is not advisable to use any of the following in any incense or ritual perfume: foxglove, deadly nightshade, hemlock, thornapple, amanita muscaria (fly agaric toadstool), black hellebore, henbane or any derivative of the white poppy.

One of the most important tools you can use in magical working, whether working on your own or with others, is incense or ritual perfume. This chapter explains why incense has such powerful properties, gives you easy-to-make recipes and suggests the most appropriate times for using them.

Again, any warnings about certain herbs or their use appear with the individual entries.

It is vital that in magical working all the elements and equipment used must be in total harmony with each other for the correct results to be achieved. If you are working with others, this includes people and apparatus, which should all harmonise with each other, giving a feeling of unity and the knowledge that what you are doing *will* have the desired intention. This applies in all magical systems including Wicca and the Quabala. The Quabala is a system of traditional knowledge based on the Hebrew alphabet (Quabalists believe that the letters have mystical meanings) and on the use of numbers to represent spiritual ideas.

Incense is important as it gives the whole proceedings

the correct 'feel', especially when you are working with deities/elementals and planetary correspondence; the incense prepares the working area's atmosphere in a way that is conducive to the invocation of a particular force or deity. It produces an environment where the forces invoked feel at ease and where they are welcome: it is their invitation to the ritual.

With incense and perfume, you create an environment where the force is happy. After all, could you live in an alien environment, such as under water, for example, without an artificial aid? Of course not, and this is why it is vital to use the correct incense for the deity invoked.

INCENSE-MAKING: A SKILLED ART

It is not a case of slapping together anything that smells good and hoping for the best. Incense-making is a skilled art. After all, the results of your working may depend upon the potency of the incense. Making incense is complicated and before deciding upon the type to be made, other considerations have to be taken into account, such as:

- the time of day, month and year
- the position of the planets
- the phase of the moon
- the harvesting of the herbs at the appropriate time
- having mixing bowls and utensils of correct planetary correspondence
- making sure that the recipes used are capable of doing what you wish them to do.

NO SHORT CUTS

As you progress with your magical education you can begin to experiment with incense and perfumes, but remember it is a specialist procedure and must be taken steadily with no short cuts. With recipes, it is highly unlikely that you will have access to coven records on incense as very few exist. It is far better to formulate your own recipes using good guides for planetary and deity correspondence of ingredients, such as Culpeper's Herbal, Crowley's *777* or my own book, *Traditional Wicca* (available from Deosil Dance

Publications; see p106). The best guide, of course, is your own common sense.

USE YOUR COMMON SENSE

Common sense is vital, for remember that, by burning, the active ingredients of the herbs, barks, oils and gums used in incenses are released and ingested by the practitioner. The degree of stimulation depends upon the ingredients used. For example, deadly nightshade is Saturnine and foxglove comes under the rulership of Venus, so no one in their right mind would consider using either of these in an incense or oil.

A lot of Grimoires (Book of Shadows – see page 19 of Introduction) give elaborate instructions as to the correct collection of herbs for magic. These long-drawn-out directions were given because they sorted out the dabbler from the serious practitioner.

GATHER YOUR INGREDIENTS . . .

When collecting herbs or other vegetation from the wild, only take as much as you need. Never use iron when harvesting, and always leave a portion of the plant intact to reproduce itself. Leave a small gift such as bread, wine or beer and most importantly, say thank you to the spirit of the woodlands, heath or wherever you obtained your bounty.

When using herbs you have collected yourself, make sure they are totally dry, or they will rot your finished incense.

THEN MIX TOGETHER

When making incense, mix all the dry ingredients together then add the essential oils to the desired potency, a little at a time. Make a note of all the ingredients and their amounts for future reference. Store all completed incense in sterile screw-top glass jars in a cool dark place for at least three months, to allow the incense to mature and blend.

Here are some examples of my own incense formulae. All are tried, tested and effective.

HORNED GOD INCENSE

1 part patchouli leaves *Pogostemon patchouli*
1 part golden rod *Solidago virgaurea*
1 part oak bark *Quercus robur*
1 part myrrh *Commiphora myrrha*
2 parts damiana *Turnera aphrodisiaca*
10 ml/2 tsp amber oil to 225g/8 oz dry herbs

Put all the dry ingredients in an earthenware bowl and cover with the essential oil. Place by an open fire to macerate (soften by soaking), but do not boil. This is to be carried out in a dark moon or a winter's Great Sabbat. The dark of the moon refers to the few days each month when no moon at all is visible in the night sky – between the last thin crescent of the waning moon and the first time the new moon appears. It is the opposite side of the cycle from the full moon.

WHITE GODDESS INCENSE

1 part orris root
1 part white rose petals
2 parts gum damar
5 ml/1 tsp jasmine oil to 225 g/8 oz dry herbs
5 ml/1 tsp neroli oil to 225 g/8 oz dry herbs

This incense should be made on the night of a new moon. Place all ingredients in a silver bowl, cover with a white cloth and leave to bathe in the light of a full moon. Leave for a full lunar cycle.

ESBAT INCENSE

An esbat is a regular meeting of a coven of witches. It includes a religious ceremony, magic, healing and the discussion of business matters. It most commonly takes place at full moon (13 times a year).

3 parts damiana *Turnera aphrodisiaca*
2 parts frankincense *Boswellia thurifera*
1 part rosemary *Rosmarinus officinalis*
2 parts gum copal
1 part spurges *Euphorbias*

Pound all the ingredients to a fine powder in a mortar and pestle. To be compounded on the night of a full moon.

Over the page are some incense recipes formulated by a number of other Wiccans.

DARK MOON INCENSE

> **Warning!**
> *Hemlock is poisonous, but much of its power is lost when dried.*

Equal parts of:
myrrh *Commiphora myrrha*
cinnamon *Cinnamomum zeylanicum*
cassia *Cinnamomum cassia*
hemlock *Conium maculatum*
Palmful of olive oil
4 drops musk oil
8 drops myrtle oil
12 drops cedar oil

❧

Powder all the ingredients. In a separate container, blend the olive oil with the musk, myrtle and cedar oil. Add to the dry ingredients and mix. Leave to dry.

Cylch Cyhiraeth

EARTH SPIRIT INCENSE

1 **eggcupful pine resin** (gathered by you from the
  tree)
1 **eggcupful frankincense**
1 **eggcupful copal**
¹/₂ **eggcupful mugwort** *Artemisia vulgaris*
¹/₂ **eggcupful vervain** *Verbena officinalis*
¹/₂ **eggcupful patchouli leaves** *Pogostemon patchouli*
¹/₂ **eggcupful oak bark** *Quercus robur*
Olive oil
Dragon's Blood powder *(Daemomorops draco)*

Grind together the pine resin, frankincense and copal.
Add the mugwort, vervain, patchouli leaves and oak
bark. Add olive oil to bind, and dry with Dragon's Blood
powder.

Spread out on parchment and leave to dry completely.
When all the moisture is gone place in a jar and bury it at a
sacred site for the length of time you feel is necessary to
empower the incense.

Cylch Cyhiraeth

NEW MOON INCENSE

*This recipe is open to interpretation regarding quantities, so use the
amounts of herbs you find effective.*

white saunders (sandalwood) *Santalum album*
lavender *Lavandula vera*
jasmine flowers *Jasminum officinale*
vervain *Verbena officinalis*
2 **pinches powdered pine resin**
Palmful of olive oil

Blend the white saunders, lavender, jasmine flowers and
vervain. Add the pine resin and olive oil. Mix and dry.

Cylch Cyhiraeth

MENSTRUATION INCENSE

*When a woman is menstruating she is very open to other worldly
influences, and her psychic centres are at their most naturally
active. This is therefore an especially useful time for projection
techniques. This recipe has been developed to celebrate women's
mysteries and to enhance those subtle magical energies for use in
psychic exercises and magical development.*

5 ml/1 tsp myrrh *Commiphora myrrha*
5 ml/1 tsp gum copal
5 ml/1 tsp red saunders (red sandalwood)
   Pterocarpus santalinus
5 ml/1 tsp juniper berries *Juniperus communis*

Grind up the juniper berries and break the gum into
small grains, then combine all ingredients.

Chris Sempers

WITCHES' SIGHT INCENSE

> **Warning!**
> *Do not inhale the fumes directly; hemlock is poisonous,*
> *though much of its poison is lost when dried. Henbane is also*
> *poisonous.*

This recipe is also open to interpretation regarding quantities, so
use the amounts of herbs you find effective.

1 eggcupful myrrh *Commiphora myrrha*
2 drops neroli oil
3 drops amber oil
5 ml/1 tsp almond oil
1 eggcupful of:
sweet sedge *Acorus calamus*
wild lettuce *Lactuca virosa*
mugwort *Artemisia vulgaris*
lobelia *Lobelia inflata*
passion flower *Passiflora incarnata*
½ eggcupful of:
damiana *Turnera aphrodisiaca*
hemlock *Conium maculatum*
henbane *Hyoscyamus niger*
red saunders (red sandalwood) *Pterocarpus*
    santalinus

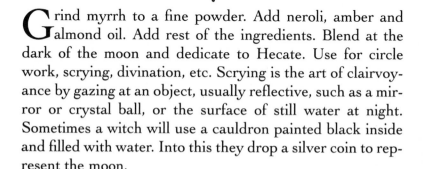

Grind myrrh to a fine powder. Add neroli, amber and almond oil. Add rest of the ingredients. Blend at the dark of the moon and dedicate to Hecate. Use for circle work, scrying, divination, etc. Scrying is the art of clairvoyance by gazing at an object, usually reflective, such as a mirror or crystal ball, or the surface of still water at night. Sometimes a witch will use a cauldron painted black inside and filled with water. Into this they drop a silver coin to represent the moon.

Cylch Cyhiraeth

RITUAL PERFUME

Ritual perfumes are used in a similar way to incense, but are applied to the bodies of those participating in magical working. The body scents of members of the group join with the natural oils and incense used to create a unique group identity.

> **25 g/1 oz incense** (use the recipes for incense)
> **25 ml/1½ tbsp sweet almond oil** (make sure it is sweet; ordinary almond oil is a diuretic!)

Place incense and oil in a small pan and heat gently. Do not boil. Keep at that level for 10 minutes, watching constantly. Let the mixture cool at room temperature. Strain and put into a sterile screw-top jar immediately.

Keep in a cool place and use within three months. If you wish to keep the perfume indefinitely, use 2 ml/¼–½ tsp benzoin to 25 ml/1½ tbsp perfume, to act as a preservative.

Abridged from *Wicca Awakens* by Keith Morgan (a Deosil Dance publication, see page 106).

BIOGRAPHIES OF CONTRIBUTING WITCHES

Some addresses and telephone numbers of the Wiccans living in Great Britain who have contributed to this book are included in the following information. Details are, of course, given with the permission of the people concerned but, in the first instance, please telephone or write, rather than call in person.

CHRIS BRAY

Chris Bray, together with his wife and partner Jude and other helpers, owns and runs the famous Sorcerer's Apprentice shop in Leeds. It is the largest occult supplier in the world, with a quarter of a million occult items in stock and a mailing list of around 60,000. It aims to provide a point of access to all aspects of the mysteries and occult, and to assist every genuine soul interested in occultism to find a magical path which suits his/her nature.

Chris Bray and his team also produce *The Lamp of Toth*, a pan-occult magazine which they aim to publish quarterly.

In 1984 the group were among those who founded the Sacred Tree Trust, a registered charity which promotes 'the aesthetic, practical and spiritual enjoyment of trees'. They plant trees in sacred groves, care for established trees that have a special spiritual/legendary importance, and disseminate information on the subject through *The Ancient View of the Tree*, a booklet available from the Sorcerer's Apprentice.

The Sorcerer's Apprentice is also responsible for the Fellowship of the Sphinx, a computerised occult network service that is available to all established clients. This enables occultists to locate like-minded people in any area of the United Kingdom, and is especially helpful when an occultist moves to a new area and wishes to contact the group already in existence there.

The Sorcerer's Apprentice Press publishes otherwise unobtainable important works on magic, for example the *Collected Works of Austin Osman Spare, The Candlemagic Spellbook, The Occult Census* and *The Beginner's Guide to Paganism, Shamanism and Witchcraft.*

The group's latest and perhaps most important enterprise is the formation of the Sub-Culture Alternatives Freedom Foundation. This has succeeded in protecting the rights of individuals to follow their own particular religion or beliefs in a climate which is sympathetic to all.

One valuable development of the Freedom Foundation's work was the establishment in 1993 of a research library to which both members and non-members donated occult books or important books that they thought should be preserved. The library has proved very useful in counteracting the disinformation put out by those who try to discredit minority beliefs.

Chris Bray and the other members of his group also maintain the Occult Register, which lists genuine people willing to be interviewed by the media.

Contact details:
Chris Bray
The Sorcerer's Apprentice
6–8 Burley Lodge Road
Leeds
LS6 1QP
Telephone: 01132 451309

LINDA BRUCE

Linda Bruce was brought up in a magical environment and had the good fortune to have a grandmother who opened her young mind to the observation of everything around her, including the world of plants. In this way her interest in herbs and their uses was triggered, and her knowledge of the subject has grown and developed all through her life.

Linda Bruce has had psychic experiences for as long as she can remember, but her real spiritual work began in 1968 when she was 20. Since then she has been involved in psychic work at several levels.

Many have benefited from her Tarot, sand and crystal readings, for this busy mother of three will always find time to give advice to someone in need of guidance. Apart from counselling, she is a talented maker of wands, charms and talismans; each is crafted especially for the person concerned. Fellow occultists recognise Linda Bruce as an unusually gifted person.

Contact details: Linda Bruce lives in Kent and works in the New Age shop 'Mind Matters' in Canterbury, where she may be contacted.

PATRICIA CROWTHER

Patricia Crowther has been a practising witch since 1960. She is a high priestess in the Gardnerian tradition of Wicca, founded by Gerald Brosseau Gardner, of whom she was a close friend. For many years she has been a leading spokesperson on witchcraft both in the UK and overseas.

Patricia Crowther was born in Sheffield, the great-grand-daughter of a Breton herbalist, clairvoyant and fortune teller. She has recalled (through hypnotism and clairvoyant visions) two past lives steeped in the Old Religion, though covering very different aspects of it. In one, she was a spell-casting old woman who lived in a hut during the seventeenth century, in the other, a priestess serving the Goddess.

Her parents taught her singing, dancing and acting, and for some years she earned her living on the stage. In 1956 she found herself performing in the same show as a magician called Arnold Crowther. He introduced her to Gerald Gardner, known as 'Britain's Chief Witch'. In due course Gardner initiated her into the Craft and shortly afterwards she initiated Arnold Crowther. Later that year Patricia and Arnold Crowther were married in a handfasting ceremony (the Wiccan marriage ceremony) – by Gerald Gardner.

The pair set up home in Sheffield, continued to learn

about the Craft from Gerald Gardner and became prominent speakers on witchcraft. They gave interviews, undertook lectures, appeared on radio and television and wrote two books together, *The Witches Speak* (Athol Publications, Douglas, Isle of Man, 1965; reprinted Samuel Weiser Inc., 1976) and *The Secrets of Ancient Witchcraft* (University Books, New Jersey, 1974). Sadly, 1974 was also the year in which Arnold Crowther died.

Patricia Crowther is the sole author of several volumes about the Craft, including her autobiography, *Witch Blood!* (House of Collectables Inc., New York, 1974) and the much-quoted *Lid Off the Cauldron* (Frederick Muller, London, 1981; reprinted Samuel Weiser Inc., New York, 1985). She continues to give public lectures, to appear on radio and TV, and has written numerous articles for occult magazines. She also enjoys keeping her hand in with stage work – especially as a magician!

CYLCH CYHIRAETH

This Cylch, the Circle of Cyhiraeth, the Welsh Goddess of Life, Streams, Rivers, Wells and Springs – essentially the Flow of Existence, is based in North Wales but has members in South Wales too. It practises a traditional Welsh Craft that is partly Druidic. It consists of an Inner Circle and an Outer Training Circle.

The recipes given by the Cylch are at least 200–300 years old. In a few cases they have been updated by the addition of essential oils.

SYLVIA GUYATT

Sylvia Guyatt spent her early years in her grandmother's house in London. She was a district nurse and midwife who taught her grand-daughter much of what she knows about herbs and their properties. When Sylvia Guyatt was six the family moved to Rayleigh, Essex, where she got to know a family of gypsies, and played with their children.

At the age of 12 the family moved to Rainham, Kent (where members of her family still live), and she continued to learn about herbs from her grandmother and mother as well as from other sources.

She married from there and moved to a 300-year-old cottage in the Hampshire village of Rowlands Castle. She has a son and daughter and now lives in Benfleet, Essex. She is a priestess of Isis and a Third Degree Wiccan, who runs a local group.

JACKIE JAMES

Jackie James, known as the 'White Witch of Brixton', was born in Camberwell, London in 1932. Her mother has magic powers and Jackie James believes it was because of these that no close relative was injured during the 1939–45 war and the family house survived the Blitz with no more damage than a few broken windows.

Later, when she was married, others began to be aware of her gifts for seeing into the future and performing other magical acts. In particular, she was able to solve problems for her children and those of friends by holding on to knotted pieces of string and willing the restrictions away.

Around this time she began reading about Wicca, and in due course entered the Craft, partly to gain more control over her magical powers. She was especially drawn to the Tarot, both to the cards and their history. She is also dedicated to the Moon Goddess Isis. Jackie James is a lone witch who does not belong to a coven or group. She deals only with other genuine people who live too far apart to form any kind of regular assembly but occasionally communicate on subjects important to them all.

She received much publicity a few years ago when she was aboard the pleasure boat *The Marchioness* which collided with another vessel in the Thames and sank. Many young people were drowned. Jackie James had been invited aboard by a friend who thought it would be a novel birthday present for their host to take a witch along to read his cards. When the boat was struck Jackie James was thrown into the water and suffered a broken leg. Only a few minutes earlier she had been giving a reading to one of the guests, which included the warning 'Do not travel by water'.

KEITH MORGAN

Keith Morgan is a Third Degree traditional Wiccan, initiated into a traditional coven and taught their ways. He has moved away from the confines of modernistic Gardnerian/Alexandrian-orienated Wicca and taken his concept of the Old Religion back to its traditional roots, in the energies and spirits of the Celtic nations of Albion, Cymru, Alba, Mannin and Eire. He lives in his spiritual homeland of Cymru with his partner Dianne and young son John.

He considers himself to be working, believing and living in the ways of the wise ones of these lands – the tribal wise men and women.

Keith Morgan is a teacher of the old ways, an author with several books under his belt and editor of *Deosil Dance*, a journal about the Old Religion.

Enquiries about *Deosil Dance* publications should be addressed to:

The Earth Spirit Lodge
Noddfa
Llithfaen
Pwllheli
Gwynedd
Wales

PAULINE NEWBERY

Pauline Newbery was part of Wicca for ten years, and is now an initiate of the Western Mysteries, whose work is concerned with magic for the Aquarian Age.

She has had a number of articles published in magazines such as *Destiny, Prediction* and the *The Inner Light Journal*. She has also appeared on Tyne-Tees Television and Anglia Television, and was featured in a film made on location in Britain for Berlin Television. The documentary was subsequently sold to several other countries.

Her psychic abilities first showed themselves before she reached school age. Her special gifts are a strong affinity with animals, with whom she can communicate telepathically, and a deep interest in herbalism and its natural curative qualities. She has been interviewed by 'sensitives' (psychics) at the College of Psychic Studies in London and found to be a very powerful 'physical medium' (one whose physical body is used to produce such psychic phenomena as automatic writing and painting, materialisation of objects etc. This includes trance mediumship (channelling), where the body of a medium is taken over by a spirit from the 'other side', wishing to send messages to this world). An account of the occurrences during this meeting, together with many other well-documented manifestations of her psychic powers, will be found in her forthcoming auto-biography *Keepers of the Key*.

Pauline Newbery lives in Kent with her husband and they have one daughter.

CHRIS SEMPERS

Chris Sempers lives in East Yorkshire with her husband Graham Raven and son Michael. She has been interested in the medicinal use and folklore of herbs and other plants since her schooldays. She grows, gathers and prepares many of her own herbs, so her house is constantly festooned with bundles of plants in various stages of drying.

A herbalist and aromatherapist, she uses herbs and essential oils in a wide variety of ways both in her home and in the mail order business she runs with her husband. Their company, Raven, supplies a very wide range of unusual, weird and wonderful, magical merchandise, much of which is handmade by the couple. Their wares include fact sheets on just about every mystical subject there is. For a free cat-alogue, write to Raven at 17 Melton Fields, Brickyard Lane, North Ferriby, East Yorkshire, HU14 3HE.

JEAN TIGHE

Jean Tighe was born in Surrey, and is a psychic consultant who from a fairly early age found she could sense past events and predict future ones for other people. She also discovered an ability to influence certain situations by the power of thought.

She started practising psychometry for friends (psy-chometry is the psychic ability to divine the history of, or events concerned with, a material object owned by a person, e.g. a ring, watch or letter), and went on to use the Tarot and rune stones as her 'tools' to focus her psychic energies. She has studied numerology and astrology, including Karmic astrology. She compiles astrotapes, which consist of the comparison of a couple's planetary positions to enable them to be aware of their compatibility level and the strengths and weaknesses of their relationship.

In 1980 Jean Tighe went to the United States, living first in Utah and then in West Virginia with her husband, a delegate to the West Virginian State legislature and later a Democratic candidate for the Senate. She returned to England in 1983 and studied at the College of Psycho-Therapists (White Lodge), in Tunbridge Wells.

She has given psychic readings for many years and regularly visits Europe to see clients. She also gives postal readings. Apart from her highly developed psychic sensitivity, she has the gift of mediumship, which she uses when called upon to help in cases of haunting and poltergeist activity.

Jean Tighe has a knowledge of Wicca and other spiritual practices, but is now a practising Buddhist. She is also involved in complementary medicine and healing, working in these areas when she is able. She also enjoys giving advice and assistance on the ancient Chinese art of Feng Shui. This promotes the free flow of Ch'i (energy) within the home or business to free blockages or stale energy, bringing about positive changes in health, wealth and happiness. Jean Tighe also enjoys giving lectures and workshops, on request.

Contact details:
Jean Tighe
7 Derwent Way
Rainham
Kent
Telephone: 01634 388648

KIM TRACEY

Kim Tracey is a noted psychic who over the years has given readings to a wide range of clients, including royalty and celebrities, using her special rune stones and amazing skills. She was once responsible for the switchboard of a radio station being jammed with incoming calls after giving advice over the air to childless couples on the best times to conceive. In due course, the tangible results of her assistance were there for all to see!

She has been aware of being gifted with the 'sight' since childhood when, during the war, she and her mother were evacuated to Scotland. A neighbouring old lady who read tea leaves took a very youthful Kim Tracey 'under her wing' and helped her to develop her powers.

When she left school, she laid aside her clairvoyant talents and drifted from job to job, a typical teenager searching for her niche. Eventually she became a singer with a small band and it was through this that – in the most extraordinary way – she was encouraged towards a career in the occult. The advice was given to her by the late, legendary Elvis Presley – also the possessor of psychic powers – whom she came to know when she was singing in a nightclub in Hamburg and he was a national serviceman stationed in West Germany.

Even then it was many years before she became a professional clairvoyant. First came marriage and the birth of her daughter, then the entry into her life via automatic handwriting of Saul, the person she describes as her 'eternal mate'. She and Saul had known each other in many previous incarnations, but in the past circumstances had always parted them. In her autobiography, *Secrets of the Runes* (1979), Kim Tracey wrote of her high hopes that in this lifetime they would at last be together, but very sadly he died from a heart attack before that became possible.

In 1975 she came to the end of a long personal journey when she discovered the ancient and mystical runic alphabet, said to have originated in Norse mythology. She made a set of rune stones for herself and became a full-time psychic. There followed a star-spangled decade of appearances on radio and television, newspaper and magazine articles, well-publicised trips overseas – and secret journeys to Kensington Palace.

Interspersed with the glamour, came a steady day-to-day stream of visitors to her home in Chatham, Kent, for the uncannily accurate personal readings she gave.

A few years ago she moved back to her beloved Scotland. Unfortunately she has of late suffered from ill-health and is now retired.

SOURCE LIST

If you have difficulty obtaining the herb seeds, dried herbs or essential oils you need locally, this section gives you information on suppliers throughout the country, where you will find a wide range on sale, including some of the rarer species.

Culpeper run 20 shops throughout England and also have a mail order department, as do the other suppliers listed.

This section also includes information on suppliers of occult books.

SUPPLIERS OF HERB SEEDS

John Chambers Wildflower Seeds
15 Westleigh Road
Barton Seagrave
Kettering
Northants
NN15 5AJ
Telephone: 01933 652562
Mail order. Very comprehensive herb section, including rare species.

Suffolk Herbs Ltd
Monks Farm
Coggeshall Road
Kelvedon
Essex
CO5 9PG
Telephone: 01376 572456

Mail order. Comprehensive catalogue, including many types of herb seeds and brief notes on their usage. Includes some interesting snippets of herbal information.

SUPPLIERS OF DRIED HERBS

Culpeper Ltd (Mail Order Department)
Hadstock Road
Linton
Cambridge
CB1 6NJ
Telephone: 01223 894054

There are also 20 Culpeper shops in England: two in London (Bruton Street and Covent Garden), and one each in Bath, Birmingham, Bournemouth, Brighton, Cambridge, Canterbury, Chester, Guildford, Leamington Spa, Lincoln, Liverpool, Norwich, Oxford, Salisbury, Sheffield, Southampton, Windsor and York.

Culpeper's mail order stock includes a large selection of dried herbs (and a good selection of essential oils).

Magistra
46 Carlisle Avenue
St Albans
Herts
AL3 5LX
Telephone: 01729 858028

Mail order. Dried herbs from a genuine Wiccan source. Also essential oils, incense burners and candles.

Neal's Yard Remedies
2 Neal's Yard
Covent Garden
London
WC2 9DP
Telephone: 0171 379 7222

Retail and mail order. The London herbal centre has an international reputation for dried herbs, essential oils, homeopathic remedies and toiletries. The Mail Order Department is in Manchester (telephone: 0161 831 7875).

Raven
17 Melton Fields
Brickyard Lane
North Ferriby
East Yorkshire
HU14 3HE
Mail order. Good list of dried herbs (and many items 'to enhance the Art Magical'). When writing in, a stamped addressed envelope would be appreciated.

The Sorcerer's Apprentice
6–8 Burley Lodge Road
Leeds
LS6 1QP
Telephone: 0113 2451309
Mail order. Very good selection of dried herbs (and many other items).

SUPPLIERS OF ESSENTIAL OILS

Culpeper Ltd – see under Suppliers of Dried Herbs
Mail order and retail.

Raven – see under Suppliers of Dried Herbs
Mail order. Good selection of essential oils; a fact sheet on aromatherapy is available.

The Sorcerer's Apprentice – see under Suppliers of Dried Herbs
Mail order. Very good selection of essential oils.

SUPPLIERS OF OCCULT BOOKS

Merlin's Cave
31 North Road
Brighton
BN1 1YB
Telephone: 01273 622859
Mail order service. Good source of occult books and goods.

Mysteries
9–11 Monmouth Street
London
WC2H 9DA
Telephone: 0171 240 3688
Mail order and retail. One of London's famous occult suppliers, for books and much else.

Occultique
73 Kettering Road
Northampton
NN1 4AW
Telephone: 01604 27727
Mail order and retail. Another large occult store, for books and all occult paraphernalia.

The Society of Metaphysicians
Archer's Court
Stonestile Lane
The Ridge
Hastings
East Sussex
TN35 4PG
Telephone: 01424 751577
Mainly mail order. Has a good selection of occult books, including many out of print.

The Sorcerer's Apprentice – see under Suppliers of Dried Herbs
Mail order. One of the country's largest occult centres. Stock includes a large number of rare occult books.

INDEX OF AILMENTS AND RECIPES

INDEX OF PLANTS